Curated Fiction

Curated Fiction presents a new theory and methodology for developing, drafting and refining creative writing. At the intersection of literary studies and creative writing, this book develops a new theory for analysing how novelists use narrative point-of-view to direct readers' trust.

The book defines the parameters and practice of one possible approach to the creative development of a work of long-form fiction. The value underpinning this approach will be drawn from the theories that inform it, such as Irene Kacandes's work on Talk Fiction, Bakhtinian concepts of polyphony and Gerald Prince's concept of the Disnarrated.

Offering critical analyses of existing literary works, such as *Waterland* and *As I Lay Dying*, *Curated Fiction* will afford examination of theory in practice, in differing literary forms and contexts before making practical connections with the craft of writing through the analysis of an original short story, 'Foxes'.

Dr Cameron Hindrum lives, writes and works in lutruwita/Tasmania, the island state of Australia. He was awarded a Doctorate of Creative Arts (Writing), with double commendation, from the University of Wollongong in 2021. His first novel, *The Blue Cathedral*, was published in 2011 and revised and reissued in 2023; his second novel, *The Sand*, won the 2022 University of Tasmania Prize for best unpublished manuscript at the 2022 Tasmanian Premier's Literary Awards.

Curated Fiction
Novel Writing in Theory and Practice

Cameron Hindrum

NEW YORK AND LONDON

First published 2024
by Routledge
605 Third Avenue, New York, NY 10158

and by Routledge
4 Park Square, Milton Park, Abingdon, Oxon, OX14 4RN

Routledge is an imprint of the Taylor & Francis Group, an informa business

© 2024 Cameron Hindrum

The right of Cameron Hindrum to be identified as author of this work has been asserted in accordance with sections 77 and 78 of the Copyright, Designs and Patents Act 1988.

All rights reserved. No part of this book may be reprinted or reproduced or utilised in any form or by any electronic, mechanical, or other means, now known or hereafter invented, including photocopying and recording, or in any information storage or retrieval system, without permission in writing from the publishers.

Trademark notice: Product or corporate names may be trademarks or registered trademarks, and are used only for identification and explanation without intent to infringe.

British Library Cataloguing-in-Publication Data
A catalogue record for this book is available from the British Library

Library of Congress Cataloging-in-Publication Data
Names: Hindrum, Cameron, 1970- author.
Title: Curated fiction : novel writing in theory and practice / Cameron Hindrum.
Description: New York, NY : Routledge, 2024. |
Includes bibliographical references and index. |
Identifiers: LCCN 2023056625 (print) | LCCN 2023056626 (ebook) | ISBN 9781032635453 (hardback) | ISBN 9781032635460 (paperback) | ISBN 9781032635477 (ebook)
Subjects: LCSH: Narration (Rhetoric) | Fiction--Authorship. | Creative writing--Technique. | Fiction--History and criticism--Theory, etc.
Classification: LCC PN3383.N35 H56 2024 (print) | LCC PN3383.N35 (ebook) | DDC 808/.036--dc23/eng/20240102
LC record available at https://lccn.loc.gov/2023056625
LC ebook record available at https://lccn.loc.gov/2023056626

ISBN: 978-1-032-63545-3 (hbk)
ISBN: 978-1-032-63546-0 (pbk)
ISBN: 978-1-032-63547-7 (ebk)

DOI: 10.4324/9781032635477

Typeset in Times New Roman
by KnowledgeWorks Global Ltd.

This book is dedicated to the first storyteller
I knew: my father, Marcus.

Contents

	Acknowledgements	*viii*
1	In Which I Vanish	1
2	Of Ghosts and Things: *Waterland* as a Narrative Black Hole	11
3	The Nature of the Goods: Absence as Provocation in Graham Swift's *Last Orders*	28
4	Strange Blood: The Anti-Language of *As I Lay Dying*	46
5	The Secret Room: Artifice and Historical Angst in *A Room Made of Leaves*	61
	Foxes	70
6	Synthesis: An Analysis of 'Foxes'	79
7	Curated Fiction in Practice	86
	Conclusion	95
	Bibliography	*96*
	Index	*99*

Acknowledgements

I am deeply indebted to the following people for various measures of support, inspiration and guidance they have provided me for either the development of this book or the doctoral work that preceded it: Dr Joshua Lobb, Professor Lisa Fletcher, Naomi Milbourne, Lucy Christopher, Danielle Wood, Robert Clarke, Rohan Wilson, Shirley Patton, Joy Elizabeth, Stan and Rebecca Gottschalk and Kathleen Austin-Gifford.

I am especially and always in debt to my wife Sonja for her wisdom and insight and to our eternally patient children, Lachie and Charly.

1 In Which I Vanish

What is Curated Fiction?

This chapter will define the concepts and practice of a narrative framework I term Curated Fiction; subsequent chapters will apply this framework to several contemporary works of fiction as well as to the practice of creative writing. This framework consists of three central elements drawn from literary or narrative theory: polyphony, a theory that written language constitutes a multitude of voices; orality, the extent to which written narrative can resemble oral communication; and one or more first-person narrations, which ideally will be ordered by a curatorial character within the storyworld—that is, the character who has made decisions about whose voice will be heard and when. These elements work to imply a clear sense of authorial distance from the work, establishing the illusion of a hermetically sealed storyworld. Such an approach establishes and maintains the illusion of authorial absence. It manifests a strong sense of verisimilitude in the narrations, which in turn objectifies the act of narrative composition: the narrations included do not appear to be the result of an omniscient authorial act. In other words, the Writer vanishes.

This chapter will also map some theoretical terrain against which the following chapters of the book will be explored. Specifically, I will provide explanations relating to authorial trust (Eco 1994), unreliable narration and objective authorship (Booth 1983), orality (Kacandes 2001), some brief contextual discussion on ambiguity (Brooks 2010) and the Bakhtinian notions of utterance and polyphony (Renfrew 2015; Emerson 1997). These concepts will not be rendered in intricate detail in this chapter; where appropriate, during the relevant subsequent chapters, the concepts and ideas sketched in this introduction will be expanded upon through the prism of their practical application.

At a functional level, Curated Fiction is the collection of multiple homodiegetic accounts of events constituting the manuscript's storyline. These accounts have ostensibly been 'commissioned' by one of the characters involved in those events, who has the role of Curator for this purpose; the Curator orders and edits the accounts, presenting them to the reader in such a way that creates the illusion of a comprehensive and balanced overall narration;

DOI: 10.4324/9781032635477-1

it is this 'process' of Curation that allows the Writer to apparently vanish from the work. As events proceed and accounts develop individual arcs for the characters providing them, biases and preferences may emerge so that the veracity of what is being related to the reader may be questioned—opening up a conversation addressing the function of truth in storytelling, and the quality of trust that can be instituted in the teller(s) of the story. In this chapter, I will discuss these elements of narrative construction and the extent to which they can generate a sense of deliberately unreliable narration.

In subsequent chapters, I will analyse how three novels (*Waterland* and *Last Orders* by Graham Swift, and *As I Lay Dying* by William Faulkner) have instituted some or all of the four elements in ways that represent Curated Fiction; I will further argue that a fourth example, *A Room Made of Leaves* by Kate Grenville, ostensibly appears to embody a framing device based on Curated Fiction but does not do so. This is because Grenville's novel, while clearly based in historical fact and on primary sources, explicitly reveals its construction to the reader at the end; Grenville has not, therefore, vanished, and instead announces—indeed, embraces—the actuality of her role. The three other novels were chosen because of their narrative multiplicity: *Waterland* employs a single narrating character who exhibits a variety of textual voices, while the other two offer discrete multiple narrators: seven in *Last Orders* and sixteen in *As I Lay Dying*. I will synthesise my reading of each novel with relevant theory to expound on broader concepts or techniques including multiple first-person narration and the propensity of Curated Fiction to institute concepts of text-as-trauma, authorial absence and ambiguity. The commonality shared by each of these novels is Curated Fiction: each employs a character or characters within the storyworld to offer specific and particular accounts to the reader, with varying degrees of authorial absence. *A Room Made of Leaves* is included in order to discuss an example of what Curated Fiction is not.

I will stress that I am offering only one such framework against which to measure, develop or reconsider the act of creative writing; in application to a specific writer's practice, this framework may be reformulated, revised, or only some parts of the framework may be of use or relevance. Nonetheless, I hope that the framework is extensive enough to offer something to writers seeking to imbue their work with some narrative complexity or compelling structure.

Curated Fiction, Unreliable Truth and the Invisible Author

In *Six Walks in the Fictional Woods* (1994), Umberto Eco argues that notions of the acceptance of truth in a fictional world compared to the actual world might be inverted. Eco states that "we read novels because they give us the comfortable notion of living in a world where the notion of truth is indisputable, while the actual world seems to be a more treacherous place" (1994, 91). I would contend that Curated Fiction displaces such a notion—that a fictional world can be equally unreliable with regard to manifestations of truth. As a consequence, the reader may navigate the various accounts and internally curated narratives of the fictional world to determine their own understanding of what is narrated.

There must be a clear correlation between curated accounts and the much broader principle of unreliable narration. Narration may be unreliable, according to Wayne Booth in *The Rhetoric of Fiction*, because the narrator "believes himself to have qualities that the author has denied him" (1983, 159). In this way, the narrator is a narrative device, creating a smaller or larger narrative distance between author and reader, depending on the extent or purpose of the unreliability. Such unreliability is explicit, however, and activates the reader in engaging directly with forming an acceptance of the truth or otherwise of events that are narrated. Narrative unreliability in the context of Curated Fiction is implicit, and this is because the "flesh-and-blood person" (Booth 2005, 76) who is the author, has established a clear distance between themselves and the narrative act through the use of a character as Curator—by whom major decisions regarding what is related, by whom and when, are made. (This can be simply summarised by considering an important trio of narrative questions, adapted from the work of Mieke Bal: Who knows? Who sees? Who speaks? I will focus on the specific function of these questions later in this book.) The narrative act is therefore complicated by creating layers of narration: an account may be rendered unreliable by faulty memory, by trauma, by the simple passing of time—or by the more sinister manipulation of received material by the Curator. In other words, instead of a singular point of view through which actions or events of a novel are presented to the reader, Curated Fiction presents several; and even within individual points of view, there may be layers of perception, insight or clarity. This requires readers to engage with the narrative at the level of choice—regarding but not limited to which account is more reliable than another, or even within individual accounts, which information is reliable and which is fanciful or digressive.

Such choices establish ethical parameters that inform an engagement with Curated Fiction. If the central events related via this framework are purported to be true, the extent to which truth is manipulated through the relation of events from multiple sources must be examined. This may occur against the degree of trust placed in either the flesh-and-blood person or the curating character to provide reliable accounts, as proposed by Eco who defines fiction as a world that "we have to take as it is, on trust" (Eco 1994, 89). While this may be true for the vast majority of centrally or singularly narrated fictional work, it is a significant generalisation when considered in the context of Curated Fiction, where the placement of trust may shift as an active part of the reading process. Curated Fiction also invites a correlation between the level of trust enacted by the reader and the level of authorial distance exhibited by the flesh-and-blood person. One such example of this is offered by the proposition that a reader is less likely to trust events related to them by someone named Cameron Hindrum, who they do not know, than by a character named Tom Crick, with whom they form a relationship as the events of *Waterland* are revealed. (In a novel such as *As I Lay Dying* where there are sixteen different narrative voices, the reader has clear choices to make regarding who is reliable and who is not—in other words, who to believe and who to regard sceptically.) The 'shift' of trust will occur in accordance with the development and growing strength of that relationship.

We can extend this understanding into a conception of what I term the objective author-self, an entity illustrated by Booth. Understanding authorial objectivity is premised firstly on Booth's admission that "though the author can to some extent choose his disguises, he can never choose to disappear" (1983, 20). What Curated Fiction strives to enact is an illusion of disappearance—ideally, as thorough an illusion as possible. Booth cites Jean-Paul Sartre, imparting fixed views on how far that illusion might be taken: "It is not enough ... that an author avoid omniscient commentary altogether ... [or] that he is sitting silently behind the scenes ... He must give the illusion that he does not exist" (1983, 50). This might suggest similarities between a narrative project and a documentary: the words constituting the novel are the words of selected people who lived through and observed the experiences and events depicted. They have not been bestowed on those people by an unknown omniscient authorial being; in other words, for example, on the characters of *Last Orders* and its readers, Graham Swift does not exist. (Except, as we shall see, that Swift complicates this notion in fascinating ways.)

Decades of narratological thought have occupied the relationship between the narrator and the narrated, between omniscience and subjectivity, between intrusion and detachment in the composition of a written sequence of events; often, somewhat simplistically, this has boiled down to a binary debate regarding mimesis or diegesis, in layman's terms, 'showing or telling'. With regard to arguing that Curated Fiction creates an illusion of authorial absence, Gerard Genette declares that "... narration, oral or written, is a fact of language, and language signifies without imitating" (Genette 1980, 164). I will expand on this further in Chapters 5 and 6. The principle I am establishing is that this illusion activates authorial absence in a work of Curated Fiction, and in turn, such absence establishes veracity and integrity as core components of the storyworld; you do not have an omniscient authorial presence that infers, 'I am making all of this up'. (I will return to this notion in more detail in Chapter 5, on Kate Grenville's novel *A Room Made of Leaves*.) In the absence of such an inference, the reader is left to accept what is narrated as truthful and authentic. In addition, first-person narration, of the kind employed in all the novels discussed in subsequent chapters, is predicated on 'telling as showing' in that subjective points of view directly relate a version of events, with any and all compilation of those events occurring within or at least emanating from the storyworld. The reception and comprehension of what is narrated are unique to those who narrate it, not mediated by an omniscient 'authorial' source; the central organising force of these narratives is curatorial, not authorial. This begins to deliver us into the realm of orality, enacting the role of spoken language in narrative, which I will define in more detail later in this chapter.

Booth's definition of the implied author also draws on the notion of 'the second self', espoused by Kathleen Tillotson. Broadly, this notion contends that the author of a book is not the person who wrote the book but a devised version of that person's self: "the 'narrator' ... is a method rather than a person; indeed, the 'narrator' is never the author as man ..." (Tillotson 1980, 22). Tillotson also notes: "When the critic objects that an author's voice 'destroys the illusion', it is surely dramatic rather than narrative illusion that he has in mind; in narrative illusion, *the teller has a rightful place* [emphasis added]" (11). Curated Fiction respects this assertion by privileging the teller (or tellers). This is established again by the deliberate placement of authorial awareness entirely within the storyworld and the conceit that only those who witnessed or directly participated in or observed the events being narrated are permitted to narrate them. However, Tillotson's distinction between the narrative of events and the drama of events is significant and may hold the key to mapping the precise role of the 'author' in Curated Fiction. While there should be the illusion of absence so that the storyworld of the fiction appears self-contained and independent of an artificial act of creation, it is tacitly understood that such an act has indeed occurred; however, while the author may be responsible for conception of the storyworld, the dramatic enactment and relation of events within that world are the sole domain of the characters, without perceived influence, comment or judgement by the author. William Faulkner's *As I Lay Dying* and Graham Swift's *Last Orders* are constructed thus: apparent authorial absence leaves characters to navigate their experiences within the story and relate them subjectively to the reader. As the chapter focusing on *Last Orders* illustrates, though, there are moments of authorial intervention, disguised and seemingly objective as they may be; this may be reinforced or complicated by appointing one character as Curator—meaning that accusations of subjectivity or privilege can be levelled at that character, further delineating a sense of actual-authorial detachment from the storyworld that is as thorough (or thoroughly illusory) as possible.

Curated Fiction closes the loop on narrative construction. It relies on narrated first-person accounts that have been curated: requested or commissioned, collated, edited and commented on by an additional narrator who is also active within the storyworld. This ostensibly blurs the line between showing and telling, which in turn activates elements of authorial absence and unreliable narration. The composite intended effect of such a construction is to underscore the entirety of the narrative project with veracity. The events that are narrated, the conflicts within and between them, and the manner in which they are presented to the reader are intended to establish a clear sense of veracity: that these events actually happened. Such veracity is an illusion, however, reinforced by the ultimate subjectivity of the act of curation; the result is an interrogation of truth, trust, and the limits of perception.

Curated Fiction and Orality

Orality encompasses the degree to which narrative acts in fiction assume oral dimensions. Such dimensions may be evident textually in the form of capturing region-specific vernacular or idiosyncratic punctuation. This is illustrated, for example, in nearly all of the different narrative voices that constitute William Faulkner's *As I Lay Dying*, and to a lesser extent in the missing punctuation mark in the word 'aint' that features consistently in the monologues of *Last Orders*. Irene Kacandes has labelled such works "talk fiction", "because they contain features that promote in readers a sense of the interaction we associate with face-to-face conversation ('talk') *and* a sense of the contrivance of this interaction ('fiction')" (Kacandes, 2001). Kacandes makes the point that such a definition not only relates to factors governing the aesthetic composition of texts but to text-reader interactions as well, in which the reader discerns a sense of being addressed and encounters a work of fiction as conversation. Questions are asked here about the line between writing and speaking as narrative acts; I can write down an account of what happened to me yesterday, which would represent a narration of those events, or I could ring a friend and tell them what happened, in which the case depiction of those events might be fundamentally different. Within the context of Curated Fiction, narration is a speech act, not a language act—not, per se, an act of literate construction, but of shaping and sequencing events based on recall or observation from within specific and clearly identified points of view that are not authorial.

Two specific elements of orality that are germane to the examples in this book are the rhetorical device of the apostrophe and second-person narration ('you-narration'). Apostrophe is defined as the turning away from one's usual audience to address someone who cannot or will not respond; it establishes a 'double-audience' (my term) and motivates the actual reader of the text to position themselves in relation to what is said and how it might influence their perception of speaker and context. Kacandes states

> the content of the message being delivered is rarely as important as the relationships created by the complicated enunciative situation. Structures of address are mobilised not to promote a verbal reply by the specified addressee (who, besides, may be incapable of speaking) but rather to *promote an emotional response in actual readers* [emphasis added].
>
> (xvi)

The potential use of such a technique in Curated Fiction is clear—where more traditional methods of narration have been displaced by multiple singular points of view and the aforementioned illusion of authorial absence, opportunities to complicate the emotional texture of provided narrative accounts deepen and enrich the integrity of the characters and to establish them as 'real'. Graham Swift employs this device for Amy's last chapter in *Last Orders*, which is addressed to her severely disabled daughter June. To underscore the profound emotional context of Amy's heartbreak at her recently deceased husband never acknowledging June's existence, her narration concludes abruptly mid-sentence: Amy simply finishes 'talking'. Orality therefore has a clear role to play in establishing a perception of truth within the narrated accounts of a work of Curated Fiction; there is no clearer method of presenting a character for judgement in a work of fiction than in the character's own words. Further, orality in narration enables emotional texture: we can establish not just what is observed but how it felt. The emotional lives of characters are, within the context of Curated Fiction, best and most accurately rendered through their subjective voices.

Concomitant with the prevalence of narration in the form of speech acts, then, is the use of second-person narration, *you*-narration, which has particular value in the context of Curated Fiction as a means of enacting empathy and instituting a sense of intimacy, if only temporarily, between the reader and depictions of or reflections on events in the fictional world (Mildorf 2016). It has a direct correlation with notions of address, and in particular, the reader must determine who is being addressed—the narrator (if the second-person perspective is provided from that of another character), the author, the reader or another character in the fictional world. The establishment of empathy is possible through the involvement with the reader that second-person narration seeks to create, as Mildorf states: "Involvement is achieved because *you*-narration employs direct address and thus creates a quasi-communicational setup with real readers" (Mildorf 2016). Such involvement is essential within the context of Curated Fiction, as it will either engage the reader with the narrative or it will help orient the reader between narrated accounts, so that interactions, attitudes (of characters to each other) or connections between accounts begin to coalesce. The distinction of a 'real' reader here is worth noting, as it illustrates the complex communicatory system within which Curated Fiction operates: an actual-author, a curator-author (who edits and organises, in this overarching narrative construct), several narrators and at least two readers—one within the storyworld (the curator-author again) and one actual, the flesh-and-blood reader of the novel. Mildorf asserts that this form of narration "lacks overt mediation through a narrator and exclusively offers us insight into the mind of a character instead" (Mildorf 2016). Curated Fiction can interrogate this claim, since some form of mediation is possible through the curator-author—although how much mediation and in what form (privileging, editing, omitting or truncating accounts) is a matter to be negotiated in the reading of the novel.

The core value of second-person narration is its enactment of empathy. Mildorf argues that "we as readers can arguably come to feel close to the character more easily, especially if his or her disposition and experiences match our own" (146). There is innate value in striving to connect readers with what is being experienced, encountered and felt in the storyworld, and second-person narration (especially when employed as a device within the wider narrative architecture of Curated Fiction) offers rich opportunities for such a connection to be at once any combination of contrived, celebrated, complicated and/or compelling.

Curated Fiction, Polyphony and Ambiguity

A clear connection that is enabled by the narrative aesthetic of Curated Fiction is between homodiegetic narration[1] (in its multiple incarnations within Curated Fiction) and Mikhail Bakhtin's concept of *polyphony* (Emerson 1997; Renfrew 2015). In the context of Bakhtin's vast contributions to literary theory, polyphony has become a central landmark. The word itself originates semantically in music, describing the presence of many voices in a choral work, for example; however, some misinterpretation of the term has evolved since Bakhtin conceived it not merely to relate to voices but ideas. The obverse position is *monologism*—that is, the entirety of a work of fiction emanating from a single, unified author-consciousness (Renfrew 2015, 77). Renfrew further states that in "monological literature of any kind ... the author is the sovereign subject of discourse, while his or her characters are merely *objects* of that discourse". Polyphony, then, rather than releasing characters from the singularity of an omniscient authorial voice, releases them from the authority of that voice and any thematic, metaphorical or symbolic constraints it might impose—in other words, it sets them ideologically free. For Bakhtin, the polyphonic novel

> is constructed not as the whole of a single consciousness, absorbing other consciousnesses as objects into itself, but as a whole formed by the interaction of several consciousnesses, none of which entirely becomes an object for the other.
>
> (Bakhtin 2013)

From the work of Fyodor Dostoevsky, Bakhtin draws the notion that a novel free of the constraints of plot cites character as 'idea-hero', "an idea that uses the hero as its carrier in order to realise its potential as an idea in the world" (Emerson 1997). One reading of such a sentiment is that Curated Fiction enacts character-driven rather than plot-driven narratives; certainly, in *Last Orders* and *As I Lay Dying*, plot is largely subservient to the development and exposition of character. In turn, this drives a fundamental sense of reader engagement, according to Caryl Emerson: "once a dialogue of ideas ... becomes the common denominator between author, hero and reader ... readers can participate actively—which is to say, non-vicariously, on an equal plane—in the narrative" (1997). Just as a reader might be positioned to evolve a trust-response in one or more of the narrators of Curated

Fiction, the reader might also connect more deeply with ideas exposed by the execution of an approach governed by Curated Fiction to relating the events of the novel. This creates rich opportunities for immersion: the reader is within the story, navigating empathies and locating themselves within the narrative, emotional and interactional terrain that the storyworld affords them.

This degree of multiplicity, derived from multiple narrative voices that establish a polyphonic narrative texture, foregrounds and may even necessitate the presence of ambiguity. David Brooks posits ambiguity as "close reading ... concerned to find what is there rather than what we wish to find there, aware at the same time that nothing is there—can be there—without us" (Brooks 2010). In this way, if we position the act of reading as a search for narrative and/or emotional truth—represented, for example, by a satisfactory sense of resolution to a story (narrative truth) or the lovers overcoming obstacles to find happiness in each other's arms (emotional truth), understanding that the two typically occur simultaneously—then truth, according to Brooks, "might come in this way to be seen as a process, rather than something abstracted from process". We can discern a connection, then between concepts of ambiguity with Bakhtinian notions of polyphony. If Bakhtin suggests that polyphony has the potential to lift the novel off the page and allow the creation of fiction to assume dimensions of integration at the level of character and speech, then ambiguity becomes prevalent as a component of the immersive world called into being as a result. Brooks argues that

> every text invokes the world ... is synechdochic of it ... in the sense that every text, opened by the kind of reading that close reading brings to it, serves as a window onto something else, something greater, beyond it ... Texts may be made of the same basic fabric, language, but they are made of many other fabrics as well—or rather, language, as language, is not the only fibre woven through them.
>
> (4)

A narrative that is conceived and composed in this way will be cast in dimensions of breadth, across a narrative of events, and depth, into narratives of character. It will question the authority of textual resolution and instead celebrate individual characters' encounters with moments of action and response. It will position the reader within the storyworld, and it will eschew authorial omniscience in favour of intimate subjectivity.

One might suggest that literature must be reclaimed for the people it celebrates: ordinary characters, drawn from life but aesthetically above it, confronted with the messy business of living. Curated Fiction is their vehicle, their means of inhabiting a world in which some semblance of control and response is returned to them, ostensibly without authorial imprimatur: a world in which, provocatively, they operate within the illusion of having some influence over what defines them and how they respond to it.

In Which I Vanish

To summarise, Curated Fiction is an overarching narrative methodology composed of multiple first-person narrations that are curated (commissioned, collated, edited and where necessary commented on) by a character who also exists within the storyworld. The illusion created using this methodology is one of authorial absence, which engages the reader by instituting the need for empathy and decision-making regarding trust and truth. Since the narrations draw on orality, the notion of spoken text captured authentically, narrations will (to varying degrees) be as revealing about the narrators as they are about their narrations, with the through-line of combined accounts representing a polyphonous assembly of different voices who respond to central important events in contradictory ways—contradictory in terms of what is narrated as well as with regard to emotional consequences. As mentioned earlier, different forms of this methodology and its features will be illustrated via discussion and analysis of four contemporary texts: *Waterland* and *Last Orders* by Graham Swift, *As I Lay Dying* by William Faulkner, and (to provide a counter-example) *A Room Made of Leaves*, by Kate Grenville.

These analyses will position Curated Fiction as a tangible, sustainable, emphatic and compelling methodology for the composition of fiction. It speaks to the very heart of fiction's role in broader artistic endeavour, to allow vicarious pleasure in sharing the lives and experiences of others, to find relatability with characters and experiences that may inform our own understanding of people or experiences, engaging with a series of events, experiences or situations from a perspective (or variety of perspectives) that is very different from our own. In so doing, at the intersection of character and story, the elemental nature of truth may be interrogated. In reading as in life, we may be required to consider who it is we choose to trust in relating experiences to us. I don't posit that this is anything new with regard to the act, the process, the composition or the joy of reading or writing—but I will argue that utilising Curated Fiction, drawing on its features, provides a compelling and provocative means of crafting such fiction.

Note

1 Please note that the term 'homodiegetic narration' is often used to denote first-person narration, whereas the scope of the term is broader than this: homodiegesis in narration simply refers to a narrator who operates within the storyworld. Subjective third-person narration (such as in, for example, *The Boy in the Striped Pyjamas*, with the exception of that novel's last couple of pages) is also homodiegetic.

2 Of Ghosts and Things

Waterland as a Narrative Black Hole

Context: The Novel

Waterland is Graham Swift's third novel, published in 1983. Importantly, it varies from my definition of Curated Fiction in one significant respect, which is that it features a single narrator, Tom Crick; however, there are distinct variations in narrative voice throughout the novel so that its overall narrative texture is dynamic. There is clear synthesis between this texture and broader emotional purpose: over the course of the novel, these two forces become so tightly interdependent that as soon as a moment of clear emotional catharsis is reached, the novel concludes; as I will argue, the narrative architecture of the novel collapses upon itself. This presents an opportunity to analyse the novel's authorial absence.

Waterland is a novel of vast scope and narrative complexity, and Swift himself has noted its publication 'marked a watershed in my career' (Swift, 2010). Significantly, Swift also identifies the new creative energy that seemed to pervade the writing of the novel—"it was 'bigger', more ambitious than anything I'd previously attempted ... I felt I could do and get away with anything."

The novel's narrator is a history teacher named Tom Crick. The premise binding the various threads of the novel together is that he terminates his planned lesson in class one day, and begins telling his students about his own past: his childhood as the son of a lock-keeper on the River Leem, his adolescent flirtations and sexual fumblings, his brother Dick who has what would now be identified as a profound learning disability, and the discovery one day of a body floating in the lock by his house. Simultaneously, *Waterland* addresses the narrative of histories and is a historical narrative which also navigates the personal; the novel explores, interrogates, deconstructs and reconstructs Tom Crick's sense of self. His delivery of personal stories to his students, which lends the novel its binding quality of orality, is initially motivated by the actions of his wife Mary, who has attempted to abduct a child from a supermarket. As teenagers, Tom and Mary were lovers; as husband and wife in adulthood, they are childless as the consequence of an abortion Mary

DOI: 10.4324/9781032635477-2

endured during her adolescence. The narrative threads of the novel dart off in many directions: the generational history of both of Tom's parents, the history of the Norfolk Fens where much of the novel is set, Tom's adolescence, the death of Freddie Parr and its cause and consequences, and so on. Much of Tom Crick's preoccupation is with a former student named Price, who provides the starkly ironic counterpoint to much of the book's narrative and thematic action with his claim that history "has got to the point where it's probably about to end" (*Waterland*, p. 14[1]). Despite this multiplicity, the novel retains masterful cohesion—one conjures the idea of Swift as conductor, calling on the various symphonic sections of his craft at appropriate moments and synthesising them.

I will analyse key scenes from the novel in this chapter in order to illustrate its adherence with the principles of Curated Fiction. The broad principles I will explore are the nexus between orality and trauma (Kacandes, 2001); the nexus between orality and authorial absence, specifically the notion of how direct address displaces omniscience and limits narrative distance (Booth, 1983); and broader concepts of ambiguity in fiction as well as Bakhtinian notions of polyphony and utterance.

Story as Redemption in *Waterland*

The intricate but immoveable narrative architecture of *Waterland* has, as its foundation, a series of apparently contradictory notions which establish some Bakhtinian parameters for the framing and exposition of the novel's story (Champion, 2003). More simply, what constitutes 'narrative' in the telling of this novel's stories, and what does not? And where do the lines of narrative and orality, of telling as opposed to writing, intersect? A close study of *Waterland* allows for some clear exploration of the concepts of Curated Fiction; the orality of the novel (and of Tom Crick's narrative voice) shifts, often markedly, creating a complex mosaic of registers, ideas and ambiguous points of view—trying to "put together a story which is made to echo with other stories, within or without" (Tollance 2008, 141). Events of the novel draw on temporality, myth, history, trauma, family lore and the ecology of the Norfolk Fens in which most of the action is set. Swift himself recognises the narrative variances he was playing with, "often shift[ing] into something not like narrative at all … I felt confident about these seeming digressions, that they wouldn't be digressions but vital parts of an organic, if idiosyncratic and complex, whole" (Swift, 2010). Swift is offering a definition of Bakhtin's concept of polyphony here; the digressions he refers to also relate to voice, language, style, and variations within and between these elements. Thus, we have a definition of the core elements of Curated Fiction: the orality of the novel's composition and the implied authorship established through Crick's first-person narration, and the sense of authorial absence that is created as a result. Swift's ability to absent himself as the author of his fiction is something we will return to in more depth in the next chapter.

Thematically, *Waterland* is concerned with Crick's attempts to find salvation for himself, his family, and his understanding of history through the stories he imparts to his students—stories as a catalyst for redemption. From the opening page of the novel we are reminded of the importance of stories to young Tom Crick: "My father ... had a knack for telling stories. Made-up stories, true stories, soothing stories, warning stories; stories with a moral or no point at all" (*Waterland*, p. 10). At its simplest, of course, *Waterland* is a story about stories and the nature of story, and it succeeds for the extent to which it generates metaphors for the presence and resilient value of stories in our lives. The novel's overarching structure is one of stories within themselves, connected by the present-day conflict facing Tom Crick as he deals with the news that his teaching career is about to be terminated. The fabric of Crick's storytelling is vast and non-linear, touching on (in one respect) the fading sense of authority Crick is experiencing in the present day of the novel. This reminds us of several contradictions that exist at the heart of *Waterland*—Crick is telling stories that he wishes had no need to be told, or certainly that he had no need to tell them.

As such, he seeks solace in the imaginary and mythical domain of those stories, and in doing so compounds one or more of the novel's central artful contradictions: imagination as a device for confronting the truth, or fiction as a site of fact. In turn, this compounds the notion of narrative subjectivity that is central to the deployment of Curated Fiction— and in the case of *Waterland*, since we only have one narrating agent through which all events are related, strong reader engagement is enacted through constant negotiations based on trust and whether we should imbue Tom Crick with appropriate narrative authority. Accordingly, Swift plays with notions of voice and absence: the novel is "made up of fragments ... and trace[s] the disappearance of an authoritative voice" (Tollance, 2008, 142). This allows us to interrogate the concept that Tom Crick is a singular narrator.

For the purposes of framing *Waterland* as an exemplar of Curated Fiction, there are two strands of critique that will be discussed here and integrated with central arguments about the thematic composition, if not the specific structure, of Curated Fiction. The first of these draws on a Bakhtinian notion of duality in the narrative voice and positions the novel as a confessional statement (Champion 2003); the second constitutes an explication of *Waterland* as trauma fiction (Whitehead 2004; Russell 2009). I argue that between these two positions, narrative space exists in which concepts of reader engagement and ethical positioning are activated, and that *Waterland* provides a rich opportunity for analysis of the central tenet of Curated Fiction—that multiple narrative voices are at work which (in this particular case) emanate from a single narrator.

Margret Gunnarsdottir Champion's analysis of the novel firmly embeds it in Bakhtinian notions of double-voiced explication: history is both objective and mythical, landscapes are both wild and tamed, humans are capable of enlightenment and darkness (Champion 2003). This sense of contradiction and complication both informs the structure of the novel and underpins its narration. Hence there is a division of point of view in the novel; in Champion's phrase, a "cracked voice that reverberates from the smallest adverb to issues of profound human significance" (2003, 41). There are elements here of 'Crick as novelist' in which he deploys the tools of narrative fiction in creating the accounts of history (both his own and the accepted histories of events such as the French Revolution)—tools such as characterisation, setting, manipulation of time and so on. There is a shaping, then, to the stories he tells, and that shaping serves a double purpose—to give some outward structure which will serve to tailor his stories for his audience (his students), and to allow Crick to order the material he is presenting for his own purposes—that is, through lenses of narrative, to provide some perspective by which he might understand the experiences that have formed him; in other words, curating them. Consequently, Crick forms his own narrative hierarchies: he departs from the information he should provide during his lessons and replaces it with information that he needs to encounter and shape in order to reclaim his sense of self:

> so when your history teacher's teachings are to be put to the test, when his wife, who is yet to be branded by the local press as 'The Baby Snatcher of Lewisham' or the 'The Child Thief of Greenwich', delivers herself one Sunday afternoon of an inexplicable announcement, he obeys both human instinct and academic training. He drops everything (even the French Revolution) and tries to explain himself. ... because it's the inexplicable that keeps him jabbering on nineteen to the dozen like this and scurrying further and further into the past.
>
> (*Waterland*, p. 113)

He places himself at the centre of the stories he tells—sooner or later, they lead back to him and the formative experiences of his youth, experiences punctuated by tragedy in the form of murder, abortion and the suicide of his older brother Dick. Champion states:

> [the] simultaneous closeness and distance of traditional history is necessary in Crick's enterprise as teacher of young people who are disenchanted with antiquarian education. In the outburst of Price, the most outspoken student, Crick recognises his own desire for identification with the 'Here and Now', for unobstructed knowledge of the present moment. ... Crick's students want to abandon the history lesson so they can meet directly the various crises in their world [of the early 1980s]—the nuclear threat, American hostages in Iran, religious and ethnic conflicts ... As an idealistic pedagogue, Crick creates a counterspeech, a double-voiced discourse or—as he often refers to it—a yarn that challenges his listeners to become ideologists themselves instead of being subjected to a deceptive ideology.
>
> (2003, 38)

Crick's telling of stories has multiple functions. By replacing traditional pedagogy with meeting an immediate and arguably more interesting need, Crick attempts to order the significant events of his own past; in addition, he activates the ideological desire of his students to recognise patterns of history as occurring in that present moment—patterns that will, from their perspective, evolve to directly influence the world in which they live and work. Swift notes that "handling the past is one of fiction's principal, perennial functions" (Swift, 2010). Crick, by these definitions, adopts a curatorial role in the sharing of his own stories.

Curated Fiction and the Explication of Trauma in *Waterland*

Narratively, the impetus for Crick to begin regaling his students is double: the disturbing behaviour of his wife Mary, who has abducted an infant from a local supermarket, as well as the likelihood that owing to various pressures, not least of them Crick's propensity to abandon the curriculum and tell stories, his teaching position has become untenable. Richard Rankin Russell (2009) posits this departure from Crick's expected duties as the clearest sign that he must navigate some profound trauma so as to cope with present-day demands and stresses, and thus the narrating of his past is a cathartic act, central to engaging with *Waterland* as a work of trauma fiction and central also to recognising catharsis as one of the motivating factors for narration in Curated Fiction.

Central to this is the reading of Tom Crick's characterisation as an embodiment of trauma. *Waterland* is narratively focused around three events: the death of Freddie Parr, the abortion Mary endures which renders her infertile, and Dick Crick's suicide. We learn that Dick, with his profound learning disability, is responsible for Freddie's death possibly out of jealousy; we also learn that Dick is the result of an incestuous relationship between their mother Helen and her father. News of this is contained in a letter which, for reasons that will be explored later, Tom reads to his brother; an apparent inability to cope with this news is what drives Dick to take his own life. These are events which have shaped Tom as an adult—of the three, the abortion appears to have had the most significant consequence since it culminates in Mary abducting a child from a supermarket; however, as critics have pointed out, Tom's guilt is a strong undercurrent in both the stories he tells, and his reasons for telling them (Acheson 2005; Meneses 2017).

Tom is profoundly wounded in the psychic sense of the word (Kacandes 2001).

> Recovery of the victim involves overcoming silence and withdrawal to witness to what happened. That is to say, the victim produces a narrative of the traumatic events. [This is] hauntingly difficult, however, because

the event that needs to be narrated may not have been experienced by the victim fully consciously in time.

(2001, p. 91)

Many traumatic incidents occur outside consciousness—"many accident or assault victims report how the mind—without conscious decision—elides the moment of impact; dissociation of experience may occur as the trauma occurs" (p. 91). Swift's narrative manifestations of Tom Crick's trauma, and Crick's attempts to be dissociative, underscore several key scenes of the novel. For example, the visit to Martha Clay (the 'Witch' who performs the abortion, *Waterland* pps. 297–307) provides evidence both of this dissociation and its utility as a narrative device. Tom Crick constantly delays the reader/audience; perhaps this is because he needs to delay confronting the inevitable fact of his own guilt and involvement or causality relating to the events he is narrating. Chapter 45, 'About the Witch', begins by introducing her and informing the reader that she made love potions and "got rid of love-children" (p. 297); this brief paragraph ends there, and then we must be told about the fen geese for a page or so, followed by a further brief delay with a rumination on love. Such delays are clearly dissociative: what follows, the narration of the act of the abortion, is difficult and confronting for Tom and therefore it is difficult for him not only to revisit it but share it with his audience. When we eventually meet Martha Clay, she is described:

that face! Small, moist, needly eyes. Leather purse of a mouth. Nose: bony (but in no way hooked). Forehead: bumpy-shiny, tobacco-hued. Hair: waxy-grey, pulled tight down to her scalp by a knot at the neck stuck through with two lengths of quill. And those cheeks! Those cheeks! They're not just round and ruddy. They're not just red. They don't merely suggest alternate and continual exposure over several decades, without any intermediate stages, to winter gales and scorching sun. They're bladders of fire. They're overripe tomatoes.

(*Waterland*, p. 300)

The shift in narrative voice within this paragraph is almost startling, ranging from the objective use of colons to separate specific features of Martha's face (almost as one might expect in a description from an autopsy) to the subjective use of poetic language to describe Martha's cheeks. This represents another level of dissociation: Crick is piecing Martha together from memory, navigating as he does so the fascination he may have for her as the local Witch, alongside the trauma implicit in the reason they require her services. The recall of Martha's appearance is fragmented, inconsistent; she is perhaps simultaneously real and imagined, and the narrative memory that Crick constructs of her must reflect both the emotional intensity of the moment of his and Mary's encounter with her, as well as substantiate the clear and long-term psychic impacts that this event had on them both. Such duality is reflected concisely in this paragraph but is representative of the narrative design of the novel: Tom Crick must navigate what is real, what is imagined and reconcile both of these with his sense of self. Martha's small house also typifies this: "we've stepped into a different world. The one where things come to a stop; one where the past will go on happening" (p. 303). The past does continue to happen for victims of trauma, until such time as an adequate healing occurs, in whatever form that may take. Curated Fiction, then, allows its characters to revisit confronting events in a way that provides (hopefully) helpful perspective and may enact a sense of coming to terms with them.

A useful metaphor to consider this a little more closely is that of a circuit, which may be either closed off or allowed to operate unimpeded, as dictated by circumstances. Kacandes uses this metaphor to enact the presence of trauma in fiction. Importantly, there can be no definitive narrative that adequately relates the events of the trauma—"no 'authoritative telling' of the event ... Rather, the presence of the analyst/co-witness/reader completes the circuit and allows the story to come into being" (*Talk Fiction*, ps. 94;96). The completed circuit creates a loop around which the story travels, being told by a narrator, received by the audience, and taken back into the self of the narrator. This 'taking back in' will constitute, one hopes, a kind of progress towards healing; the process of sharing the traumatic event will give it shape and perspective so that the narrator is able to find something in it of value. This is not to say that the telling of stories will, in and of itself, allow healing to occur, and one of the central questions in *Waterland* asks whether or not Tom Crick achieves any sort of satisfactory resolution as a result of sharing his stories with his students—who are, effectively, his co-witnesses or 'readers'. Tom's mother Helen makes the point most clearly: "No, don't forget. Don't erase it. You can't erase it. But make it into a story" (*Waterland* ps. 225–6). This intersection between orality, the explication of trauma and the underlying element of polyphony underpins the architecture of Curated Fiction. A significant narrative/dramatic outcome is delay, in the sense that a resolution to Crick's dilemmas are postponed: through polyphonous narration in which profound emotional and moral conflicts are embedded, Swift unifies his narrative project by creating junctions, allowing Tom Crick to digress in order to avoid confronting the emotional truths he seeks. This intersection between polyphony and the explication of trauma invites further dissection.

Richard Rankin Russell cites the term "re-remembering", which "refers to an almost inevitable recollection of events haunting persons involved in trauma who have forgotten what they originally remembered about the atrocities" (Russell 2009, p. 117). Crick undergoes this process because as Russell states, he "cannot now cope with the present" (p. 117). Russell cites Cathy Carruth: "it is 'at the specific point at which knowing and not knowing intersect that the language of literature and the psychoanalytic theory of traumatic experience precisely meet'" (p. 118); this creates "a 'double telling, the oscillation between a crisis of death and the correlative crisis of life: between the story of the unbearable nature of an event and the story of the unbearable nature of its survival.'" The aforementioned delays, then, are in fact suppressions and the ability/opportunity to suppress is another cornerstone of Curated Fiction. Crick cannot face what he must narrate; he procrastinates. This creates several narrative effects, the clearest of which is tension—as readers (as students in Crick's history class) we are made to wait: a hallmark of Swift's work in *Waterland* is that it enacts patience. Therefore, a further narrative effect that is created is temporal: narratively, *Waterland* has a vertical axis relating to the present moment, and several horizontal ones that intersect at different points relating to the various timeframes that Tom casts out like fishing lines over the waters of his beloved Fens. This illustrates the novel's nexus between its explication of trauma and its construction as Curated Fiction: essentially, the telling of stories assumes a therapeutic dimension (Konkol 2014). Stories provide a structure for memory and thus a way to relive or retrieve those memories, reinforcing the "value of narrativisation [as] a domestication of the inexpressible experience without denying its irreducibly traumatic character" (p. 108). It is important to recognise, especially with regard to Curated Fiction, that this does not presume that healing will naturally follow. In narrative terms, healing might equate to resolution; however, if one of the central forces at work in Curated Fiction is ambiguity, healing may not be explicitly possible. Tom Crick might recognise this, in "his justification of his family's tendency to resort to storytelling as a means of overcoming a sense of fear and powerlessness" (p. 112). Overcoming is not strictly the same as healing—rather, it is a 'dealing with' or a means of putting a traumatic experience into some form of perspective so as to make it somehow bearable in the context of having to live a hopefully stable life. Therefore, and importantly, Curated Fiction has the potential to activate ambiguity as a valid component of narrative structure.

Waterland as Narrative and Anti-Narrative

The narrative architecture of *Waterland* is such that it spends much of its duration threatening to collapse (and finally does so with the suicide of Dick Crick). The delay of this collapse is perhaps the novel's most astonishing narrative achievement, and it is created by what Pascal Tollance identifies as the

> profound division where the need to tell comes into conflict with the reluctance to do so ... [it is a] narrative at war with itself, torn between the tempting, soothing voice of the tale ('Once Upon a Time...') and the voice of a discourse which analyses, dissects and takes things apart.
>
> (2008, p. 144)

In part, this is reinforced by authorial absence: Crick is in charge of this narrative and so it sings and whispers, falters and fulminates as he requires. Swift vanishes with the result that his absence enacts a space into which voices must go—so that *Waterland* becomes a sort of echo chamber with Tom Crick providing the single voice which resonates. His words, according to Tollance, "become a means of cracking the prison of the self" (p. 142). I will return to the notion of *Waterland* as a slowly collapsing narrative; I will now further explicate *Waterland* as utterance, drawing on Bakhtin's concept of polyphony as it relates to Tom Crick as enunciator.

As discussed earlier, polyphony does not merely suggest that a multitude of voices are present within a text; it allows for voices to occupy multiple consciousnesses (Renfrew 2015, p. 78). The natural extension of the polyphonic is into the dialogic: "all meaning is, for Bakhtin, dialogic; the dialogic is characteristic of all verbalised human interaction" (p. 79). Importantly, Tollance explains that "Polyphony does not only consist in a multiplication of voices; it is what breaks the unity of each individual voice and blurs the source of enunciation" (Tollance 2008, 147). The singular voice in *Waterland* is repeatedly fractured, distorted or it engages in a sort of mimicry. As an example, let us return to the aforementioned chapter 'About the Witch':

> Down Mary's leg two sudden unfurling ribbons of blood, one outpacing the other, smeared by the swish of the long grass. We stop, for a wincing pause. Anticipatory visions: spilt onto the marsh grass, a bloody tadpole, a gooey sheep's heart. Is it going to—? Now? Christ, Mary, if we're stuck out here in the dark. Twilight thickening. The time of owls and will-o'-the-wisps. Right time to arrive at a witch's. Hold my hand, Mary. Hold on, Mary. Love you, Mary. Keep going, Mary. Are we going to get there? (Do we want to get there?)
>
> (*Waterland*, p. 299)

As with the earlier cited example from this section, Swift employs a clear narrative shift to represent Tom in an anxious state of mind regarding what is about to happen (the abortion). This shift both explicates the notion of trauma and illustrates the narrative voice splintering into several strands: one descriptive ('unfurling ribbons of blood'), one full of dread and possibly disgust ('Anticipatory visions…'), one fearful ('Christ, Mary, if we're stuck out here in the dark…') and one supportive ('Love you, Mary. Keep going, Mary…') The parenthetical question that concludes this paragraph is also notable: Crick addresses his deeper self, confronting an ultimate fear of the unknown. It provides excellent evidence of the nature of Crick's larger narrative act—reluctance to tell, in conflict with the innate need to.

Tollance cites Jacques Ranciere from his work *La Parole Muette* (*The Silent Word*) to articulate how the written word is considered orphaned, "and as a result is free to journey in a way live speech cannot" (Tollance 2008, p. 148). This contradiction—that what is fixed on the page is also free–feeds into Crick's narrative dilemma and further illuminates his telling. Ranicere argues that

> Writing is ... a specific mode of enunciation and circulation of words and knowledge—the mode of orphaned enunciation, where words speak all by themselves, careless of their origin and unconcerned about their addressee ... The visibility and availability of the written word blur the notion of legitimate belonging: the utterance is no longer attached to one enunciator, one recipient or one particular mode of reception.
>
> (2008, p. 152)

There are two threads of analysis here. Firstly, the notion of 'utterance' relates both to Bakhtin's model of self-other relations as 'transposed' by Voloshinov (Renfrew, 2015) as well as to Kacandes' model of Talk Fiction. Among other things, Voloshinov's transposition presents us with "theory of the essentially social nature of language, which locates the utterance at the heart of an endless matrix of social interactions which are present in varying degrees in the act and moment of speech" (p. 74). In the section from *Waterland* cited above, interactions are clearly present, yet they emanate from a single source—Tom Crick—who is interacting with the emotional and narrative complexity of this moment in his and Mary's story. He is effectively making his own history in this moment and that history is emerging from a heavily fractured self: Tom as adolescent, as lover, as guardian, as human, as deeply fearful. If we concur with Ranciere, we can afford Mary some narrative agency here as well—although she does not speak, she is interacting with Tom through the clear pain she is in, and the resulting concern that he expresses for her. It is also worth remembering that the events of this moment in the novel, the visit to Martha Clay, directly influence both of them for the rest of their lives—indeed, the abortion is a catalyst (since it renders Mary infertile) for the act which lands them in serious trouble in the narrative present of the novel: Mary's abduction of a baby at a supermarket. Swift renders the significance of this moment through narrative abundance—almost overloading Tom with perception, emotion, insight. This notion of utterance evolves into understanding dialogism—Bakhtin's theory derived from his reading of Dostoevsky—which, according to Alistair Renfrew,

> brings to the fore something that is an almost universal phenomenon, permeating all human speech and all relationships and manifestations of human life, everything that has meaning and significance ... the dialogic is characteristic of *all verbalised human interaction.*
>
> (p. 79, emphasis added)

This narrative abundance, and the multivocality through which it is conveyed to the reader, signals a core principle of Curated Fiction in *Waterland*, despite its single narrator: the narration is varied and digressive and at times, not entirely to be trusted. In addition, Tom Crick is interacting narratively with his sense of self as it has evolved historically and emotionally, through the prism of trauma; he is, as a narrator, a point of dialogic, dramatic and narrative intersection.

This notion of 'the interactional' is crucial to reading *Waterland* as a work of orality and therefore considering it as a work of Curated Fiction. Tom Crick is, often simultaneously, talking to himself, his students, or other characters, and through all of these interactions he addresses the reader. In many cases, this address is mediated directly through second-person narration. Kacandes identifies three aspects of such interaction and the third of these, participants' perceptions of what is going on (*Talk Fiction,* p. 3), is most relevant to this analysis of *Waterland* as oral text. If, narratively, the novel is a long and disjointed attempt at unifying history and memory, its medium is talk; if talk requires perception, then we can identify Tom Crick's journey through his traumatic past as his attempt, with varying successes, to unify his sense of self: to understand who he is and how he became. In other words, talking makes memory tangible, however briefly—and once something is tangible it can be analysed. This demonstrates the novel's complexity—it is a labyrinth, through which the reader treads with some trepidation, perhaps unwinding a ball of thread as Theseus did, to help find our way out again. However, we do not need to find our way out; instead, with the suicide of Dick Crick, the labyrinth collapses.

Curated Fiction and Complexity

Narrative has become a highly subjective entity. There must be omissions; the complexity of human behaviour and thought, of motivation and insight, is such that true omniscience is nearly impossible to achieve. This is especially so with regard to narrating historical events. In this sense, Tom Crick acts as a historian who might, according to Acheson,

> survey an array of past events, select those most relevant to his purpose, then form them into a factual narrative. ... No single account of what has happened over a single period can possibly be definitive. There are too many events to be investigated, too many events that are unknown, too many ways of selecting the events, and too many ways of interpreting the selections.
>
> (2010, p. 90)

The complexity of *Waterland*, despite being cloaked in fiction, aligns with such a description. However, this assessment also provides a characterisation of the nature of Curated Fiction, which does not have a singular narrator. Even with its single narrator, *Waterland* achieves such complexity. Omniscient narration seems to have fallen out of favour over the course of the twentieth century, although it is possible to mingle omniscient narration with the subjective multiple narrative framework of Curated Fiction, as William Faulkner demonstrates in *As I Lay Dying*. The first-person narrator seems, according to Acheson, more suited to our times: "the first-person narrator is an ostensible human being, a man or woman who is unable to write with godlike authority" (p. 91). Swift seems to eschew 'narrator-as-god' status in *Waterland* in favour of bestowing full narrative authority on Tom Crick—and since Crick is narrating events as a means of processing trauma, that narrative is fractured and fragmentary. Coexisting with Crick's trauma is a clear sense of guilt—narrating to seek redemption, as an act of constructing one's own forgiveness. When Crick begins to regale his students with stories of his own life, especially that part of it involving his history with Mary, he is doing so necessarily— it is cathartic, Acheson explains, while simultaneously defining the narration itself:

> Crick distractedly relates the story of their friendship, courtship and marriage, without reference to any documents (not even letters apparently). This means that whatever he tells his students and whatever conclusions he reaches on the subject of his guilt are *not based on source materials that* other researchers could examine and form opinions about, but on his *highly subjective memories* of their shared life together.
>
> (p. 92, emphases added)

When it becomes too traumatic for Crick to address events, he digresses into a wide variety of other topics such as eels and the French Revolution. Notions of ambiguity underscore Crick's willingness (or deeper need) to digress and in the specific case of *Waterland* this ambiguity establishes Crick's shortcomings as a narrator and as a character in his own narration; it also illustrates the difficulty of intertwining history (where facts can be empirically derived from evidence) and fiction. This difficulty is also what makes ambiguity such a compelling device in Curated Fiction. Despite Crick's innate need for clarity, it continually eludes him; partly because of the passage of time, and partly perhaps because of the nature of recalling traumatic events and the propensity for details to be elided from the mind, as discussed earlier. Recalling that the catalyst for Crick's narration is his wife's abduction of a baby, Crick "can never be finally certain of the extent to which he is guilty of motivating the abduction" (98). Mary's sterility is a consequence of the abortion performed on her by Martha Clay; the unwanted pregnancy is one source of the ambiguity being explicated here. Readers may infer that Crick is the father, and Mary leads him to believe so; however, Acheson points out that "it is clear to the reader that Mary may be lying to keep him from feeling jealous of the other two boys [his brother Dick and Freddie Parr] … however, neither Crick nor the reader has any way of knowing whether she was lying ... And this is what troubles him, indeed has unbalanced him" (p. 98). A clear principle of Curated Fiction is evident: that of the reader deciding in whom they can place their trust, which in turn activates the reader as a participant of sorts in the story-world. As illustration, here is an exchange between Tom and Mary, in which he seeks some certainty about the paternity of the baby Mary is carrying. Mary asserts that it is not Freddie Parr, and that it could not be Dick

> because he didn't know how, in any case. He thought you could have one just by thinking about it. He thought you could have one—just by loving.
> Which still keeps me guessing. Because I don't believe that if Dick didn't know how, Mary wouldn't have taught him. Wasn't that why Dick made his evening trips to the Lode? To be taught? Why Mary and I took pity? Poor Dick, who wasn't allowed to be educated...Poor Dick, who wanted to know about love. That, and Mary's itching curiosity. Which has suddenly gone.
>
> (*Waterland*, p. 64)

Mary's curiosity is in reference to the size of Dick's penis, which is reported to be substantial—so much so that just prior to this exchange, Mary reported that "it was too big ... to go in" (64). The ambiguity I refer to is inherent in that curiosity having disappeared, leading the reader to suspect that in fact an encounter of some sort has occurred between Dick and Mary; the use of ambiguity in this particular case allows Tom to shield himself from what might be an uncomfortable truth.

Whether or not Crick deserves our sympathy is equally ambiguous, according to Acheson:

> In placing his guilt in a larger context, Crick is trying to minimise its importance.
> Yet, in sympathising with those who take comfort in make-believe, he is seeking to persuade us that he is ultimately a likeable figure—one who can tolerate the weakness for make-believe of uneducated people like his wife and father.
>
> (2005, 99)

Whether Crick succeeds in this mission is outside the scope of this thesis: I am more concerned with his construction as a narrator here, and issues of reliability or ambiguity inherent within that construction. Tom Crick's narration veers between jovial banter and moral panic—the latter is apparent in the previously cited sections of the novel relating to his and Mary's visit to Martha Clay—and this reflects his psychic state, the need for a chipper outward presentation that he attempts in masking some deeply felt and highly resonant tragedies. Such a balancing act is not sustainable; the tipping point is Dick's suicide at the end of the novel. Tom Crick's narration, then, is simultaneously marked by the seemingly contradictory notions of disassembly and admission and these tensions pull him, emotionally and dramatically, in different directions for most of the novel. Acts of curation—of selection and choice in what is revealed, and how, and by extension how revelation of important details are delayed—allow this tension to be sustained. In deciding, as Acheson suggests, whether or not Crick deserves our sympathy (2005, 99), we are also deciding on the larger question of whether or not we can fully trust him, and this illustrates how concepts of ambiguity and delay inherent in Curated Fiction work to complicate truth and trust in the intricate web of reader-storyworld interconnections.

Curated Fiction and the Tipping Point

I have established that this grand narrative project is built on shaky emotional territory for Tom Crick. Through enactment of ambiguity, the structuring of delay, an awareness of dialogism and an application of orality in specifically texturing the narrative, Curated Fiction is explicated as an ideal vehicle for the framing of such territory. Freddie's death, along with Mary's abortion and Dick Crick's suicide, are the triumvirate that his narration seeks to explicate. This reading positions Crick's guilt and his search for redemption centrally in what is happening, why Crick is narrating and what he is attempting to achieve for himself. Juan Meneses argues that "In appealing to its pervasive nature and relentless propensity to return, however, the narrative reveals once again Crick's reproduction of the very principles against which it is meant to work" (Meneses 2017, 141). The character of Dick Crick and his death provides us with another means by which this can be illustrated. Dick cannot read or write and can barely speak—and when he does it is in a "sort of baby language" (*Waterland*, p. 34). His silence in the novel precludes him from asking questions, from being curious, and therefore from getting in the way of Tom's carefully crafted version of his own history. Despite his silence, Dick has a crucial role to play in the narrative architecture of this novel as the one who brings everything undone. If his functional silence provides the necessary counterbalance to Crick's narrating, then according to Meneses, the latter can frame his own account as an altruistic and valiant effort to counter the historical invisibility of the family ... he can present his effort as a moral exercise of solidarity, portraying Dick as the victim of his own inarticulacy, an individual who would seek to attain historical relevance had he the linguistic means to do so. (Meneses 2017, p. 144)

This might be interpreted as Tom telling Dick's story (intermingled with all the others) because Dick can't. Although Dick contrasts Tom's narration with his silence, and perhaps Tom's intellect with Dick's lack of an intellect, Dick is effectively 'neither' in terms of the novel's land/water duality; as a result, as Meneses states, "Crick must employ his narrative dexterity to malign his half-brother relentlessly so that he can characterise him as an individual to be redeemed in spite of his ungrateful ignorance" (p. 145). As we have seen, however, his motivation on that front may be dubious, since he is merely attempting to expiate his own guilt (146). For this reason, Dick Crick's suicide can be read as the terminal point of Tom Crick's narrative project—not only literally, since it occurs at the end of the novel, but morally as well. By diving into the River Ouse, Dick abruptly truncates Tom's attempt at redemption, both on behalf of his brother and for himself. If the central purpose of his stories is to somehow make sense of his own history, Dick's death creates a point of absurdity which renders his purposes nearly meaningless, since Dick's self-destruction is an act that cannot be subjectively narrated and which is difficult to rationalise historically. Essentially, the heart of Crick's narration is a negative narrative space, threatening to implode at any moment, with the layer upon layer of story, moment, time, history, anecdote, fact, theory, reflection and reportage intricately stacked on top of one another until such time as one element—Dick's suicide—provides the tipping point, collapsing everything inwards. His death is, therefore, an 'anti-narrative gesture' (p. 147)—allowing me to conclusively tease out the two elements of *Waterland* that identify it as an example of Curated Fiction: the function of narrative as vehicle for the explication of trauma, and the potential for explicitly polyphonous narrative structures to create ambiguity and/or moral complexity. It is highly significant that the novel ends abruptly with Dick's suicide; we are not returned to the narrative present, to Tom Crick addressing his students, for any kind of satisfactory resolution. Meneses states that 'by uncoupling a sense of closure and a sense of an ending, *Waterland* unveils how Crick finally loses control over the past; he becomes incapable of containing it narratively' (p. 146). Because we are only ever subject to Tom's narration in *Waterland*, as fractured and discordant as it may sometimes be, he cannot penetrate the dramatic or narrative reality of his brother's suicide. Therefore, in the same way as Crick's capricious student Price bemoans the end of history, Dick's death signals the end of narrative—almost as if, having recalled the event, Tom-as-Narrator is unable to fully process it. This brings us back to the central tension that marks the core narrative structure of the novel: the need to recall, recall-as-catharsis, set against the trauma invoked by doing so. Even then, according to Richard Rankin Russell, Crick detaches himself from the severity of the suicide by "overlaying it with a mythical, ineluctable quality" (Russell 2009, p. 121). Dick takes his own life by flinging himself into the River Ouse from the side of a dredge called the *Rosa II*:

> for a moment he perches, poises, teeters on the rail, the dull glow of the western sky behind him. And then he plunges. In a long, reaching, powerful arc. Sufficiently long and reaching to quite discount the later theory that he must have become entangled in the anchor-chain or the sling-lines; sufficiently reaching and powerful enough for us to observe his body, in

its flight through the air, form a seemingly limbless continuum, so that an expert on diving might have judged that here indeed was a natural, here indeed was a fish of a man.

And punctures the water, with scarcely a splash. And is gone.

(*Waterland*, p. 353–4)

Significantly, the concluding section of the novel is in present tense. There is an irony here in an event from Tom's past—a memory, effectively—being rendered this way and this provides further evidence of the manner in which *Waterland* plays with time. It is also structurally significant that this is the concluding moment of the novel; as such, it is afforded considerable agency in the context of Tom's narration-as-catharsis which clearly infers that this moment is the singular event that lives and breathes at the core of Tom's guilt. In this one graceful account of a tragic event, several strands of the novel's narrative project are explicated; it punctuates the abrupt ending of the novel, coalescing symbol, myth and time—elements that have rippled along under the surface of events leading up to this moment, unified as the singular moment of Tom Crick's adolescence, a moment that provides core impetus for his need to regale his students with these and other stories during the novel's narrative present. Because of its potential for variance, this coalescence of elements demonstrates Curated Fiction's ability to operate on multiple narrative levels, in potentially contrasting voices, to establish contradictory emotional states that may defy resolution; crucially, we are reminded that one of the central narrative forces enacted by Curated Fiction is ambiguity, and the apparently contradictory power of it to provoke connection where none seems logically to be found.

Conclusion

Waterland provides clear insight into the construction of a narrative using multiple voices that emanate from a singular source; this creates some innate contrasts and contradictions that can serve as the central foundation of Curated Fiction. Tom Crick is both the subject of his stories, and the object of them; he is narrating his own stories (and, generationally, those of his forebears) while simultaneously charting the influence that stories have had on him; how it has shaped his sense of self, in much the same way as a river charts its own course to the sea, according to Tollance, "voice has become a means to achieve a form of dispossession which is simultaneously asserted and resisted in *Waterland* through Tom's loud, yet silent, performance" (2008, p. 147). This loud/silent dichotomy manifests in the central construction of *Waterland* as a trauma fiction, whereby Tom's narration acts cathartically as a vehicle for his addressing the profound moments of his making— his adolescent sexual awakening with Mary Metcalf, the death of Freddie Parr, the suicide of his brother. These three events, and Tom's reactions to them, take 350 pages to explicate and in doing so, Tom deviates considerably and consistently from 'the matter at hand', explaining why Mary abducted a baby. It is also worth remembering that, early in the novel, Tom loses his job as a history teacher, hence his sense of freedom in departing from teaching the curriculum to regaling his students with stories instead; in doing so he traces the development of his sense of self, through which the novel becomes a layered, complex, dynamic narrative. To refer to the metaphor of this chapter's title, Tom Crick's trauma creates a vast narrative vacuum: everything is drawn inexorably into it, distorting and distending Crick's emotional complexity in the process. In *Waterland* stories seem to work against themselves, acting as digressions and distractions, until we reach the moment where such functions are no longer possible, at which point Tom's function as a narrator and his act of catharsis must end; there is no more to be said. Ending the novel with the historical moment of Dick's death creates a final irony: if the novel's central motif is water, which rises and falls or ebbs and flows in cycles, then the narrative structure of *Waterland* is not ultimately cyclical. We are not returned to the narrative present for any satisfactory sense of a resolution. Ultimately, this reinforces the central power of ambiguity in Curated Fiction: that such resolutions are artificial, and that 'real life' does not always conveniently provide them. Instead, we leave Tom Crick, at the moment of the birth of his existential crisis, gazing across the water at his brother's abandoned motorbike: an empirical symbol, clearly at odds with the vagaries of the heart and the complexities of Story.

In the next chapter I will examine the confluence between multiple narrative voices and the ability of Curated Fiction to create the illusion of authorial absence, further complicating notions of narrative trust and truth, providing further evidence of Curated Fiction's complex role as a method of provocative complication.

Note

1 All page references relate to the 2010 Picador edition of the novel, with new introduction by Graham Swift.

3 The Nature of the Goods
Absence as Provocation in Graham Swift's *Last Orders*

Context: The Novel

Last Orders was published in 1996. Its events take place over a single day on which four friends meet to convey the ashes of Jack Dodds, a recently retired butcher who has succumbed to stomach cancer, to the seaside town of Margate where the deceased man requested to have his ashes scattered off the pier. The four friends, and Jack, constitute the central characters of the book: Ray, a former insurance clerk with a gift for wagering on the horses; Lenny, a market grocer; Vic, the undertaker; and Vince, Jack and Amy Dodds's adopted son, who has built a thriving car sales business from very humble beginnings. Indeed, the trip to Margate takes place in a blue Mercedes that Vince is hoping to sell to an affluent customer, Mr Hussein, to stave off a recent downturn in business. Significantly, Jack's wife Amy declines the invitation to join them.

Over the course the day, all four characters take turns to narrate the events of the drive to Margate. Numerous connections and dilemmas are revealed: Lenny's daughter Sally was once a prospective romance for Vince; Jack borrowed a large sum of money to keep his business afloat, meaning that Amy may be left with nothing after his death; Amy and Jack's only child, June, is sequestered permanently in a nursing home having been born with severe disabilities, including the inability to speak; Ray's wife Carol left him, and his daughter Susan has moved to Australia; another young woman that Jack and Amy took in, Mandy, does become involved with Vince; Ray and Amy commence an affair which continues on the days when Amy regularly visits June. Jack never acknowledges June after her birth and does not do so on his deathbed despite Amy's fervent wish. Ray, Lenny and Jack all have wartime experiences in North Africa or the Middle East in common; Vic served in the Navy; Vince also joined the army to escape Jack's destiny for him, to take on the butchery business (which is named Jack Dodds & Son).

The trip to Margate is in many ways underscored by the duality of Jack being present and not present: his ashes, in a plastic container in a shopping bag, cannot possibly represent the Jack that each man knew and loved, in his own way. As I shall discuss later, this duality is a central creative force in the novel, as Swift negotiates a narrative landscape of presence, absence, and silence. It is important to clearly embed the distinction between presence and absence as it is embodied by the character of Jack, as it mirrors Swift's authorial absence—a central concept in the context of Curated Fiction. In strictly narrative terms—that is, the sequence of events that unfolds during the novel—Jack is the catalyst for everything that happens, since the purpose of the trip to Margate (and the dramas that ensue or are recollected en route) is to honour his wish for disposal of his ashes. As noted, his ashes are present constantly: carried around by one or the other of the men or held by one of them in the car, always passed between them with utmost care and a sense of gravity; and living Jack is a constant presence in the minds and memories of the men carrying out this journey. If one of the novel's overriding concerns is the nature and composition of community, and the moral ambiguity inherent therein, then the novel's final passage can be read as a validation of absence:

> …the ash that I carried in my hands, which was the Jack who once walked around, is carried away by the wind, is whirled away by the wind till the ash becomes wind and the wind becomes Jack what we're made of.
> (*Last Orders*, ps. 294–5)

This chapter will address and analyse the key elements of the narration and structure of *Last Orders*, contextualising these within critical conversations that the novel has initiated, before closely analysing those specific attributes of the novel that align with aforementioned notions of Curated Fiction. In addition to authorial absence, these include multiple first-person narrations and polyphony in the specific voices of narrating characters. I will expand on these elements as they are evident in Swift's novel, in preparation for subsequent close analysis of key sections of *Last Orders* to demonstrate Swift's role in crafting the novel, and how this positions the novel as an exemplar of Curated Fiction. I will argue that Swift 'hides in plain sight' as the author of this work; the initial readerly impression is that the characters speak for themselves and the various narrative threads unfold organically as a result of this. It becomes clear though, specifically when Jack Dodds is given a brief monologue postmortem close to the end of the novel, that Swift's authorial role is a little more complex; and since there is an absence of any organising principle or method regarding the sequencing of the chapters we may assume that this is also a consequence of Swift's authorial imprimatur. Curated Fiction coheres the parts of a narrative structure and their underpinning concepts through a semblance of unification, and this chapter will interrogate the extent to which that sense of unification (rendered ironic by the illusion of authorial absence) is present in Swift's novel. Analysis of *Last Orders* will allow me to present it as a strong example of one of the guiding principles of Curated Fiction, namely that there must be an illusion of objectivity—that the characters, situations and sequences of the novel seem (at least initially, in this case) to exist and are presented without connection to or influence from an authorial consciousness that is external to the storyworld.

Curated Fiction and Creating Selves

It is relevant to begin this section with a brief comparison of *Waterland* and *Last Orders*, given that they are constructed in distinctly different ways yet offer some moments of clear insight into authorial choices that I have imbued with significance in terms of Curated Fiction. To frame this in terms that I return to later in this chapter, the audience is present in *Waterland* but notably absent in *Last Orders*. As Pascale Tollance suggests, "Both novels are born out of the desire to break the silence surrounding ghosts whilst turning their narrators themselves into ghostly presences" (Tollance 2008, p. 142). In terms of Curated Fiction, we can identify that the audience of the storyworld is also within the storyworld; perhaps the men of *Last Orders*, and its two women, are addressing each other. If there is a common tonality to their monologues, it is confessional. The closed-loop aesthetic that serves Curated Fiction necessarily demands that if there is no teller or narrator existing externally to that storyworld, then there is no external listener/audience either; while Tom Crick may be essentially solitary in his narrative pursuit, *Last Orders* offers a small chorus of apparently disembodied voices which, according to Tollance, "build a space where everyone is made of the other, spoken by the other and where words become a means of cracking the prison of the self" (p. 142). To illustrate, Vince is reflecting here on trips he took as a child with his father in Jack's work van:

> Then he'd go round and start the engine and I'd start to hate him. I'd hate him and hate the meat smell till they were one and the same. ... I'd lie there on the rug hating him and I'd think, I ain't going to be a butcher never, it ain't what I'm going to be. And as I lay there hating him I discovered something else, beyond and beneath the meat smell, something that made those journeys bearable. I'd put my ear to the rug. I'd feel the metal throbbing underneath ... the thrum of the shafts taking the power to the wheels, and I'd think, This is how a motor works, I'm lying on the workings of this van. I ain't me, I'm part of this van.
>
> (*Last Orders*, p. 63)

In accounts such as this one, we see Vince (in this case) in the process of creating self: his relationship with Jack is problematic and Vince does not follow his father into the family trade, instead forging his own career repairing and selling motor cars. Swift captures the moment here when Vince diverges from his father, a profound moment that will shape the rest of Vince's life, and does so by having Vince merge his sense of identity with the inanimate mechanical workings of the van. Thus, Vince cracks himself open, to utilise Tollance's phrase: he is repulsed by the sensory associations of his father's trade, and lulled instead by the almost sensual experience of lying on the floor of the van, listening to its engine and feeling its vibrations. Consequently, he shrugs off the chains of expectation or familial loyalty and begins crafting a new self, unaware of the tension that this doubleness, the dichotomy of his path in life contrasting with Jack's plans for him, will create.

Such doubleness is compelling in *Last Orders*: in addition to Vince, two of the men who convey Jack's ashes to Margate had at one stage or another a desire to be something other than they had become: as well as Vince making his own opportunities, Lenny had dreams of middleweight boxing and Ray aspired to be a jockey. These revelations evolve gradually over the course of the novel as, slowly, the men are revealed in their substance and with their faults. This is yet another distinct feature of the novel being constructed through multiple viewpoints in this way—it allows for the exposition of character in a measured way that is fragmented but continuous.

It is important to note that ostensibly, the reason they can be called monologues at all is because we can consider them spoken, not written; although, as Tollance notes, "they elude all description. They appear from the start as 'neither spoken, nor written, but mysteriously captured and transmitted'" (Tollance 2008, 148). While being 'mysteriously captured' would allow some explanation regarding the presence of Jack's voice among those of the living, I will predicate the necessary discussion here on the basis that the accounts included in *Last Orders* are explicitly oral in nature. We can consider the role of these monologues as drivers of the narrative events and as markers of identity. Importantly, it is conceivable that identities merge as this novel progresses—metaphorically at least, as suggested by the earlier citation of its closing lines; complexity lies not in its multitude of voices or their respective claims for understanding and empathy, but rather in the detachment from self that each of these voices seeks to create as the novel's events progress. In this way, traditional character is sometimes supplanted, and at most times Swift's quartet of Bermondsey chaps hover between flesh-and-blood imposition on the page, and the more ethereal realm of voice, in what Tollance describes as "a process which detaches everyone from some other which nevertheless remains a part of themselves" (149). Again, we have dichotomy at work: in the very fabric of this novel, we find constant reminders of the duality of lives—of living as an act of continual resistance that is also an act defined consistently by the power of consequence. Curated Fiction as an organising principle foregrounds this duality: in allowing characters to speak without judgement, the narrative functions and the emotional lives of those characters are both enabled. In addition, we can see the influence of Mikhail Bakhtin at work here; in his dissection of Dostoevsky's novels, Bakhtin identifies "an idea-hero, an idea that uses the hero as its carrier in order to realize its potential as an idea in the world. The goal then becomes to free up the hero from 'plot' ... from events in ordinary, necessity-driven, benumbing everyday life" (Emerson 1997, 127). Swift's ensemble of men in *Last Orders* therefore reflect a central quality that is available to characters in Curated Fiction, in that they exist both as narrative agents and exemplars of self. They occupy a space outside formal notions of fictional characterisation; their importance in the fiction lies at least as much in what they discover about themselves rather than what they achieve in terms of propelling the story.

Importantly, this coheres Curated Fiction's ability to catalyse moral behaviour in characters or textual constructions in alignment with Eco's notion of fiction as an ethical site of truth. This emanates from the extent to which varied accounts of narrative incidents are truthful (and the reasons why they are not) and converging in an understanding of how Curated Fiction creates different possibilities for interaction between trauma and memory, and the need for this interaction to motivate specific actions that might be considered self-preservation.

Curated Fiction and Moral Texture

Jane de Gay argues that *Last Orders* directly addresses spiritual questions of the insignificance of humanity against the larger, unknowable scale of life, and that—specifically in the characters of Jack and June—Swift invites us to consider how complete a human has to be in order to qualify morally as a person (de Gay 2013, 566). In pragmatic terms, Jack is deceased when the novel opens (yet, as previously discussed, remains amorphously present throughout its events, tangibly as ashes and emotionally in characters' memories); his and Amy's daughter, June, is completely marginalised by her profound disability, to the extent that she is removed from Jack and Amy's care at birth. Jack refuses to acknowledge her and never mentions her again; on the day the four men travel to Margate to scatter his ashes, Amy visits June at the nursing home where she resides one last time, to effectively say goodbye. Jane de Gay suggests that *Last Orders* poses vital questions about comparing a person who is recently deceased with someone who is completely unable to communicate in any meaningful, easily recognisable fashion. In doing so, the novel asks "about human life and human dignity and asks how anyone can be 'complete' as a human being" (566). This sense of 'completeness' adds further complexity to the narrative texture of the novel and arises almost directly out of Swift's decision to enlist more than half-a-dozen narrators. There are some intrinsic layers to each character's moral imprint; for this reason, the ultimately simple and straightforward delivery of a man's last wishes becomes entangled in myriad ways. A source of contention among the four men is why Jack chose Margate; significantly, the reason is indirectly linked to June. On their honeymoon, after June was born and had been removed, Jack won a teddy bear at a shooting gallery there—while Amy is stooping to tie her shoelace, he throws the bear off the end of the jetty as a rejection of their disabled child.

Amy realises that in fact Jack would have preferred to have his ashes cast off the jetty, but this no longer exists so he chooses the nearby harbour wall. However, it seems that this is a final, symbolic/ironic act of penance on Jack's part—a way of seeking Amy's forgiveness for his neglect of their daughter; or it may be, from Amy's perspective, a final insult, a comprehensive reminder from Jack of his rejection of June. Curated Fiction has propensity for truth to be distorted for myriad reasons, some of which may not be resolved.

Curated Fiction allows for the establishment of place in a physical and a moral sense. Complicit in the ideological fabric of the storyworld of *Last Orders* is the innate connection that characters have with each other and with the place in which those connections have evolved. While some connections are tenuous and some dysfunctional, the central thematic impulse of the novel suggests that such connections are the core of our being (an idea, again, perhaps reflected in the quasi-spiritual overtones of the novel's closing sentence)—so that we are, at once, individual and collective entities, governed by selfish desires but ultimately motivated by a sense of belonging to something beyond our selves—a circle of friends, a place of employment, a suburban community or a blend of all of these and others besides. In order for this sense of connection to exist—and, if it exists, to be beneficial—requires the practice of sympathy: of fellow-feeling, of relation to other, an acceptance of and tolerance towards not only difference, but behaviour that we might find initially find objectionable. Stef Craps (2003) interrogates this notion in *Last Orders* to derive a reading of the novel that observes the facility of its artifice; a significant plank of Craps's critique, to which I will return in the next section, is that the notion of authorial absence in *Last Orders* is not is pervasive and consistent as it might initially seem. However, of immediate interest is observing the extension of the moral calibre of Swift's characters into ethical actions, or the recognition of and accounting for unethical actions, and the extent to which parameters of Curated Fiction can directly enact such extension or recognition.

A common thread which unites every major character in the book is that they either come to terms with their past, or seek to make amends for past wrongs through a change of habit or a readjustment of values, or both. Ray determines to reunite with his estranged daughter in Australia, and debates whether to keep the money he won for Jack to use for this purpose; Vince scrabbles together a thousand pounds to provide Jack with one last act of charity (which in turn serves to clear his conscience); Lenny, less convincingly, also ponders visiting his daughter Sally, having made a sort of peace with his role in organising an abortion of the baby she conceived with Vince. Amy is perhaps the least stable of them all when we leave her in the novel, having determined that she will no longer visit June, and struggling with how she can farewell both her daughter and her husband in the same week. Of these resolutions, Ray's is the most morally problematic: he has won over thirty thousand pounds, at Jack's request, betting on a horse with the thousand pounds Vince loaned his adopted father. Since Jack dies on the afternoon the bet is actually placed, only Ray is left knowing of the money's existence, and ambiguously ponders whether he could use it to travel to Australia to see his daughter again—'no one need know' (*Last Orders*, p. 283)—or whether he should meet Jack's original intention for the money and provide it to Amy in lieu of Jack's retirement savings (of which there are none, owing to a dubious loan he organised to keep his butcher's business solvent in the years before he retired). It is strongly inferred that he will give the money to Amy, and in so doing so, according to Craps, he is elevated to "embody the ideals of love, interhuman contact and hope for a better world" (Craps 2003, 407). Such a decision, to connect with previous points of discussion, also suggests that Ray's sense of self is resolved at the closure of the novel; that perhaps more than other characters, he is settled into a course of mutually rewarding action that may offer closure to some significant emotional impediments—a long-lasting and sincere affection for Amy, and a healing of the rift with Susan, his daughter. This enacts differentiation between narrative voices: we relate to Ray on a different basis to other characters who offer their individual perspectives (and who may not, as Ray does, achieve such a satisfactory resolution); in addition, we recognise each of the narrating characters in a holistic sense, with acknowledgement of their flaws and foibles possible alongside the vicarious pleasure we can take in their emotional triumphs. The multiplicity of Curated Fiction allows for such complications, ambiguities, and resolutions—which reflect, ultimately, life's combinations of circumstances and attitudes that can establish or dismantle our acceptance of our own actions or those of others.

Case Studies of Curated Fiction in Last Orders

I will now focus on selected moments from the novel to provide close analysis of how the concepts related above, and other concepts aligned with the framework of Curated Fiction, are active within those moments. In particular, I will discuss two brief but distinct chapters of note—the shortest chapter in the novel, Vince's two-word epithet (*Last Orders*, p. 130) and 'Ray's Rules' (p. 202). I will then closely examine selected sections from the sequence of chapters in which the four men visit Canterbury Cathedral (ps. 192–226), the closing section of Amy's final chapter (p. 278) and the one chapter attributed to Jack (p. 285). Each of these moments will be discussed in terms of constructions of polyphony, of their contribution to Swift's supposed narrative intentions (for these are arguably contradictory, as I shall discuss) and more broadly as a contribution to an evolving understanding of Curated Fiction.

Vince's Two-Word Chapter/'Ray's Rules'

Since they both represent a distinct variation from the norm in different ways, let us first consider 'Ray's Rules' and Vince's two-word chapter. When we encounter Vince's brief interjection ('Old buggers', *Last Orders*, p. 130) the men are gathered, at Vic's request, at a Naval Memorial in Chatham, which represents a digression for the party from their mission with Jack's ashes. Lenny and Vince exchanged heated words at their previous stop, a pub, and tensions are elevated. However, it is ambiguous who Vince might be referring to with this brief statement—whether it is frustration with his travelling party, who are all 20–30 years older than he, or something approaching mock affection for the names of the Naval personnel lost in action, who are inscribed on the memorial. Among the four members of the travelling party, Vince stands out—as the youngest, as the only one with a direct family connection to Jack (albeit via adoption) and the only one apparently struggling to find comfort or success in adulthood. Since the novel is entirely conceived as a series of effectively spoken utterances, speech becomes Swift's only method of revealing character and so, with the ambiguity of this particular utterance, we encounter Vince as someone who remains unsure: of himself, his past or his sense of self. He projects this doubt into the casual dismissal inherent in those two simple words, which may be either insulting or genially mocking, but which are polyphonous for this reason.

In similar terms of addressing speech as character, 'Ray's Rules' reduce the luck that Ray has repeatedly exhibited in betting on horses to a series of eight axioms:

1   It's not the wins, it's the value.
2   It's not the betting, it's the knowing when not to.
3   It's not the nags, it's the other punters.
4   Old horses don't do new tricks.
5   Always look at the ears, and keep your own twitched.
6   Never bet shorter than three to one.
7   Never bet more than five percent of your kitty, except about five times in your life.
8   You can blow all the rules if you're Lucky. (*Last Orders*, p. 202).

Significantly, five are negative and the last is self-contradictory and somewhat comically self-referential; the capital L in Rule 8 signifies Ray referring to himself by the nickname bestowed on him by his peers. There is a narrative lightness to the inclusion of this list in the accounts of the journey to Margate—on one reading it is Swift shifting tone briefly, offering respite and therefore altering the rhythm of the work. Ray's fortunes as a prolific punter are an example of the narrative shape and metaphorical richness of *Last Orders*. By its nature, gambling seems to work against the sense of fatalism that otherwise pervades the novel. Ray has perfected his wagering technique over time; narratively, as discussed earlier, his gambling offers a moral complication that offsets the resolution of the novel's events for him; but even then we are reminded of perhaps Swift's most eloquent argument with this work, that lives which may appear to be simple or uncluttered by dilemma are usually, gloriously, neither. An additional function of this chapter, and especially the eighth rule, is delineated by Terrell Tebbetts in a discussion on the function of identity in *Last Orders*:

> [the characters] seem to live in a kind of trickle-down intellectual economy, picking up small change from larger intellectual exchanges. As they sift through the myriad possibilities, they actually experience the instability of identity central to the larger exchanges. ...[They] come upon an epistemology of identity offering them not a return to an unachievable stability but, instead, a fluid means of control in a shifting cosmos.
> That epistemology centres on language.
>   (Tebbets, 2010, p. 70)

An additional function can therefore be determined in 'Ray's Rules' as an articulation of self against the apparently random forces of luck and chance. Consequently, the eighth rule takes on a special ironic resonance as a result: Ray has spent most of his life living within the rules of social norms and familial expectations; developing the facility and experience required to 'break the rules' seems to serve Ray as an essential reminder of his humanity.

So multiple narrative, symbolic and textual functions are imposed on the architecture of the novel by this inclusion: the reduction of an arcane and often fortuitous process to ritual, a codification of the means by which Ray, being anything but lucky, maximises his chances of success and therefore is often granted the opportunity to provide material monetary assistance to his friends (further solidifying his sense of purpose and self); while a lightly-confected change of pace by which Swift simultaneously diverts our attention from the otherwise funereal tone of the novel and creates a moment of distraction. Such moments are always within reach under the auspices of Curated Fiction; the editorial conceit is such that digression is often feasible and compelling side-stories or changes of tone in order to fracture consistency and create interest or ambiguity are not only accessible according to the central tenet of the form (allowing characters to speak for themselves), but often necessary in order to maintain a truly rich and complex narrative fabric.

Canterbury Cathedral

The section of the novel that relates a quick visit by the men to Canterbury Cathedral also provides evidence for casting Curated Fiction as an agent of structure as well as voice. Structurally this visit occurs at about the two-thirds mark and so in dramatic terms this sequence might be said to usher in the third act and thus commences rising the action towards expected or unexpected revelations—or in one case, no revelation at all. This sequence also serves to underscore ideas relating to identity and redemption that inflect the novel. In terms of the novel's imagery, the language accompanying the dispersal of

Jack's ashes might also have its thematic origins in the visit to Canterbury. Like other concepts that Swift addresses in this novel, religion is both present and absent; in a storyworld where no one professes explicitly to practice religion, a religious current nevertheless pervades the novel.

The sequence is framed in the novel by two sections titled 'Canterbury', and these—like all of the chapters headed by a specific location on the journey—are narrated by Ray, which is why his presence in Swift's pantheon of characters is significant—he is given markedly more 'on stage' time. I will look at extracts from three of the accounts that are related while the four men are at Canterbury, in the order in which they appear: from Vince (*Last Orders*, p. 199), Lenny (p. 203) and Ray (p. 207). Vince, recalling his viewing of Jack's body in the hospital morgue, makes this reflection:

> I went through the opening and stood beside him. It smelt cold. I thought, He don't know I'm here, he can't ever know I'm here. Unless. I thought, He aint [sic] Jack Dodds, no more than I'm Vince Dodds. Because nobody aint nobody. Because nobody aint more than just a body, than just their own body, which aint nobody.
>
> Except you can't see his body under that tablecloth.
>
> (*Last* Orders, p. 199)

This brief excerpt illustrates two significant points, the first relating to Swift's use of distinct first-person language patterns and the second embedding this scene within a wider thematic context of the novel relating to self and identity. Swift's utilisation of first-person narration—a favoured technique of his since, as he notes, "I don't want to have that elevated, omniscient role; I'd much rather feel that I am down on the ground with the characters in the sort of thick of things" (Swift 1988, cited in Craps 2003, 408)—achieves special intimacy here as there can be few moments more disquieting and deeply personal than viewing a loved one post-mortem. Vince is somewhat conflicted about the role Jack has played in his life—ostensibly a fatherhood role but apparently without any of the security or support that would normally inhabit such a role. Some interpretations of his utterance here are possible then: he is emotionally ambivalent about the reality that Jack has died, and perhaps starkly confronted, not unreasonably, with the sudden realness of Jack's corpse; this is reflected in the abrupt objective observation ('It smelt cold'), and inconsistent syntax, from a single word ('Unless') to the rolling chain-of-thought rambling nature of the second last sentence cited above. I would argue that the word 'Unless' also has a significant semantic role to play here, and it invites the continuation of an intellectual inquiry by the reader—unless what? Jack is not really dead? He is dead but is watching events now from a spiritual realm? We are at once presented with a character attempting to process emotionally significant but conflicting factors that have sought to define him for almost the entirety of his own existence, and reconcile them with what he understands life to be at that point.

This scene also illustrates again the intriguing role, that of being actively absent, bestowed by Swift upon Jack. He retains relevance in death—he continues to inspire conflict, reflection, sympathy and love, all underscored by the sense of community out of which his last journey to Margate emanates; while in pragmatic terms, the novel is a flowchart of sorts that measures Jack's reduction—from a living being to a terminally ill man to a corpse (as here), to finally, in the novel's last moment, a nebulous cloud of ash. Here Curated Fiction might borrow something from the realm of magical realism—it steps, as a narrative construct, outside the bounds of immediate perception and in doing so activates further ambiguity. Perhaps most beneficially, it simultaneously suggests and precludes an authorial role in the novel, an act which further generates tension and complication within the design of the narrative project.

Lenny's reflections allow us to see into yet another overarching concept that is both thematic and structural, relating to fatherhood. Lenny's enmity with Vince, which boils over into a fistfight when the trip has detoured yet again to Wicks Farm, stems from Vince's almost-romantic relationship with Lenny's daughter Sally who becomes pregnant as a consequence.

> It was Vincy's doing in the first place but it was me who said, when she came right out with it and said she wanted to have the baby, 'No you don't, my girl.' My first fully weighed-up response as a father, words just shot from my gob. She said he'd come back and do right by her. I said, 'Don't talk bollocks, girl. What book've you been reading?' And she ain't ever forgiven me since.
>
> (*Last Orders*, p. 203)

Semantic constructions such as those evident add to an overall impression that Lenny is leaning on a bar over a pint, relating this to you. Since there is no context for address in the novel, no central reader-concept or audience for these monologues, perhaps Swift has sought to create exactly that impression—that after everything in the novel was resolved, the chaps all went to the Coach and Horses and took turns relating their versions of events. This feeds directly into my central conception of how Curated Fiction is organised narratively: that the characters have been asked to provide their own versions of events which are then sequenced by an additional character or an entity who can be largely invisible to the reader.

This is a moment of crystallised emotional crisis for Lenny, and by his admission it is not a scene that he necessarily handled effectively (although this depends on how you read 'words just shot from my gob'—which may carry a subtext that seems to add, 'I'm such an idiot', or alternatively might be an expression of something approaching surprise at how easy it was to assert authority in this potentially provocative situation). Whether this evocation of fatherhood is problematic or not, it speaks simultaneously to the motif of fatherhood in the novel as well as to an irony in the central decision Swift has apparently made in crafting the novel—which is to remove himself from an authorial role. In terms of authorial consciousness, on one reading, *Last Orders* itself has no father. However, as Wayne Booth argues,

> by the kind of silence he maintains ... the author can achieve effects which would be difficult or impossible if he allowed himself or a reliable spokesman to speak directly or authoritatively to us. The most frequently discussed of these effects is... the air of naturalness that is thought to be given by an 'authorless' work.
>
> (Booth, 1983, p. 273)

In terms of Curated Fiction this implies that narrative events are presented mostly without judgement and that consequently readers must actively engage with the narration at the level of deciding which events are reliably related, which characters are trustworthy and so on, recalling Eco's claim that we must take fictional worlds on trust, as cited in Chapter 1. Curated Fiction, by its design, blurs the distinction between trust and truth.

Ray's relatively short chapter is a departure from the two previously mentioned for two significant reasons; where Vince and Lenny look back on key moments in the respective contexts of their personal histories, Ray looks forward—although, before he does that, he stares into the abyss of the cathedral ceiling:

> It smells of stone and space and oldness. The pillars go up and up, then they fan out like they're not pillars any more, they've let go of their own weight and it's not stone any more, it's not material. It's like wings up there, arching and reaching, and I know you're supposed to gaze up and think it's amazing and feel yourself being raised up too, and I'm gazing, I'm peering, I'm staring hard, but I can't see it, I can't make it out. The next world.
>
> (*Last Orders*, p. 207)

This reflection represents something of a change of tone for Ray; he has been jovial and pragmatic up to this point and here he senses the presence of something much larger than himself—although, typically in the milieu of anti-sentiment Swift has established for these characters, he seems to reject it—or at the very least it remains invisible to him, unreachable and beyond his perception. But Ray here is on the cusp of the physical and spiritual realm, and the spiritual undertones of the novel are something that Swift has created seemingly without construction: that is, given the aforementioned absence of an omniscient author, his characters must encounter spiritual or religious beliefs purely on their own terms. This observation of Ray's also references the duality of this day's mission—it has a tangible, pragmatic focus (scattering the ashes) but this is accompanied by an ageless spiritual ritual, of conveying

Jack into the afterlife—'the next world'. This is given focal perspective in Ray's noticing that something clear and present in reality— the pillars—cease being pillars as they rise into the void of the ceiling—they're 'not stone anymore'. More broadly, if *Last Orders* is an account from multiple perspectives of a physical journey, then it is also the account of multiple journeys, some of which—as Ray illustrates—are metaphysical or existential. Perhaps, in this small moment of reflection in a vast and sacred silent space, Ray is travelling without moving, to coin a phrase—except that he cannot attain the ultimate insight that such an experience might afford, for reasons perhaps of the novel's comic nature or of the rational parameters of Ray's phlegmatic, working-class no-nonsense background. In this instance, Curated Fiction enacts a sense of dramatic irony—that a reader might connect with Ray at a compassionate level and recognise that he may never attain the insight he desires, ultimately casting him as a tragic figure. This is possible because Ray is not commented on authorially and any judgement made of his actions or perceptions will be at the reader's discretion.

Ray continues in this chapter to think forward (where, as noted, other characters have worked retrospectively in this sequence). He addresses his own mortality, a not unreasonable prospect given the business of the day, and supposes that he will travel to see his daughter in Australia to save her the trouble of having to return to England, when the time comes that he is not long for the world: 'When. If'. (*Last Orders*, p. 207). He even addresses, rather casually, the prospect of his own interment—'God knows where I'll get shoved' (p. 207) but foreshadows later reflections regarding his daughter and how important it would be for him to reconnect with her after many years of estrangement—'But I could save her the trouble' (p. 207), by which he means travelling to Sydney to be with her when he dies rather than having her return to him.

Ray is the character who comes closest to an act of redemption at the end, resolving to provide his substantial race winnings to Amy as Jack had requested, instead of keeping them. Perhaps the seed of this desire to be redeemed is born in this quiet moment, when Ray breaks with the narrative pattern of this novel and looks not forward or backward, but up—and in doing so, into himself.

Amy

The final two case studies allow specific analysis of Swift's creative methods relating to how this novel is narrated. The two sections I wish to interrogate are Amy's final chapter, specifically its conclusion (*Last Orders*, 278) and Jack's 'post-mortem' chapter (285)—although, as we will learn, it does not focus on him and is largely not in his own voice, but that of his father. Through these interrogations I will discuss the extent of Swift's 'active absence' as the author of this novel, positing this as a central concept of Curated Fiction, and how the aesthetic-narrative choices made in composing these two sections speak to the larger narrative and thematic architecture of the novel.

Jack has died of cancer several days prior to the narrative present of *Last Orders*, although he features prominently in the retrospective accounts that many of the characters relate as the novel progresses, in some cases going back decades. This technique is provocative because it invites a consideration of address: who are these chapters being related to? In addition, how does such a technique slot into an otherwise relatively conventional multiple-first-person narrative? For example, if Swift had wanted the reader to know that Jack's father had an important message about wastage in the butcher trade (which is what Jack's chapter solely presents), it seems feasible that one of the other characters—Vince or Amy, for example—might have included reference to it in one of their chapters. In considering why Jack has his own chapter, we are able to effectively interrogate the notion of authorial absence in the novel—and by extension, refine the use of such an aesthetic principle within the context of Curated Fiction.

Emotionally, Amy is in some despair over the decision she has made to stop visiting her severely disabled daughter—her last visit (so she pledges) occurring on the same day that Jack's ashes are being escorted to Margate. There is escalating tension present in her language and attitude, exemplifying that "Voice then ... [is] an ultimate barrier against something which is all too real—so much so that it might seem unreal—but which either way is endowed with frightful power" (Tollance 2008, p. 144). It is significant in light of the notion of address in this novel that Amy addresses this chapter to June. It begins with a heartfelt and heartbroken realisation:

> And the most I've wanted, the most I've hoped in fifty years, believe me I've never asked the earth, is that you should have looked at me, just once, and said, 'Mum'. It isn't much to have wished, all this time. Damn it, you're fifty years old. You should've fled the nest by now, you shouldn't want me around, you should be leading a life of your own. ... I've tried to know what it's like to be you.
>
> (*Last Orders*, p. 274)

Yet again, as with many of the fatherly roles in this novel, parental affiliations are either complicated or disconnected; in this case, however, unlike the male characters, the situation is beyond Amy's control and it is something she has bravely endured (on her own) in order to try and maintain her much-desired mantle of motherhood. It is significant that a short while later she equates Jack and June in her mind—in fifty years, June has made no progress in her emotional or cognitive development, and now that Jack is deceased, no further change or progress is possible for him either. Amy also notes that even when alive, Jack was not likely to change dramatically—like the other central male characters of Bermondsey who are exhibited in *Last Orders*, he was a creature of clearly fixed routines and cemented expectations: "So what was true of you, girl, was true of him" (p. 275). The use of you-narration in this chapter also separates it from the rest of the novel's voices, creating an intimate tone in which a bereft and now widowed mother is addressing her unreachable daughter. The effect is at once insightful and confronting; in a sense, Amy unravels during this chapter, charting increasingly confronting emotional terrain that builds towards the end with this final truncated paragraph, with which Amy's presence in the novel concludes:

> I've got to be my own woman now. But I couldn't have just stopped coming without saying it to your face: goodbye June. And I couldn't have said the one thing without saying the other. It won't mean anything to you but someone's got to tell you, no one else is going to. That your own daddy, who never came to see you, who you never knew because he never wanted to know you, that your own daddy
>
> (p. 278)

The implication is that Amy cannot bring herself to the final moment of closure, to reveal to her daughter that her husband has died—or it may be that the two disclosures coming so close together, farewell to the daughter and the husband, are simply too much to bear. Narratively this truncation raises interesting questions that complicate the authorial absence Swift has engineered throughout this novel. Evidence for that absence in this case comes with the abrupt termination of speech mid-sentence—for whatever reason, Amy has simply stopped talking. That this is taking place in the narrative present of the novel also allows a consideration of just how it is these various accounts and voices have been assembled; yet, as Tollance makes clear, the very fact that they have been assembled certifies an authorial presence (Tollance, 2008, p. 142).

Amy's sentence terminating in this way raises the spectre of ambiguity. We are given enough information in what she has disclosed to be able to infer both what the remainder of the sentence might have expressed, and where the resolutions disclosed in this chapter might have taken her, given that we do not hear from her again after this moment. Regardless of these possibilities, the termination is still abrupt, and it jars in a novel where other voices have been conversational, mostly jovial, chatting as if holding court at the Coach and Horses as intimated earlier. With this conclusion of Amy's presence we are given a point of departure from the expositional norm of the novel and as I have made clear with other analyses offered in this chapter it is both thematically and diegetically significant that Amy should suddenly and unexpectedly be consumed by narrative silence. (The diegetic significance emanates from 'blurring the line' between authorial presence and absence; it is Amy who has been unable to complete her sentence, but Swift who has curated this effect.) It is discomforting and unsettling, no doubt, but it illuminates a centrally compelling tenet of Curated Fiction in exemplifying the deep dichotomy at work, manifest in the tension over to what extent the narrative material is manipulated which in turn is governed by the extent to which the reader determines whether or not the curating agent—the authorial presence—can itself be trusted.

Jack

Typically, the one chapter bearing Jack's name—while it is related by him—does not belong to him but his father. I say typically because it serves as another reminder of Jack's simultaneous presence and absence in the fabric of the novel. That we hear from Jack at all is also a departure from the narrative norm that has so far been established, so it is significant that Jack's chapter appears very close to the end, when rhythm and expectation have been well established only to be disrupted. Critical responses to the novel, by Stef Craps for example, have noted this and recognise its potential as a complicating factor in the narrative:

> the inclusion of the impossible utterance of a dead man constitutes a radical departure from the verisimilitude that the novel seemed to be so anxious to preserve. The novel calls readers' attention to the fact that what he or she is witnessing is not raw reality, but mediated reality, a representation carefully crafted by the author.
>
> (Craps, 2003, p. 411)

I would question the unequivocal nature of the first statement here: since we have no evidence regarding external contextual factors relating to these voices (such as address, with the exception of Amy aforementioned) then we cannot satisfactorily conclude when, how or where they were captured. Swift has clearly decided that such information is unnecessary, preferring instead to both let his characters simply speak more or less for themselves and for readers to make up their own minds as to other factors; but without it, it is a little severe to describe Jack's utterance as impossible.

That issue aside, there is metaphorical significance in both the inclusion of Jack's voice and the content of what he imparts. It is a working-class sermon on how a good butcher will generate a thriving business by keeping a close eye on what is discarded (and with one or two elisions, this is Jack's chapter almost in entirety):

> He said, "Jack boy, it's all down to wastage. What you've got to understand is that what comes into the shop aint what goes out. Whole art of butchery's in avoiding wastage. ... If you take away the weight of the wastage from what you buy in and divide what's left into what you paid, that'll give you your real cost to set against your takings and don't you

ever forget it. ... And ending up, because of poor keeping or poor cutting, with lots of measly scraps of meat that aint fit to sell to no one'll cost you more than anything. ... What you've got to understand is the nature of the goods. Which is perishable."

(*Last Orders*, p. 285)

I am interested primarily in the location of this chapter towards the end of the novel, and how this works structurally as we reach the denouément of the journey and the casting away of Jack's ashes; I am also interested in the deep metaphorical resonance of this chapter, relating to that which is perishable; as a verbatim account of his father's advice, it is also a fitting exemplar of narrated voice, returning us to considerations of orality within the context of Curated Fiction.

Jack's chapter further foregrounds this as a technique of Curated Fiction. Jack has retained these words of his father, and insofar as Swift has assembled the accounts that constitute the novel as a whole, he has placed Jack's chapter deliberately within the novel's framework to create a specific sense of disruption to an otherwise established narrative pattern. As noted, there are dramatic, metaphoric, and symbolic reasons for this. However, if all of the chapters in *Last Orders* are speech acts, then (and perhaps ironically, coming as it does from a deceased character) Jack's chapter is the only actually spoken, as in verbatim, account in the novel. This alone affords Jack special significance and confirms his crucial role not only in the narrative events that are related, but also in the authenticity of the voices that Swift has manipulated—it simultaneously creates and signifies the dramatic effect of his absence among the voices of the living. It provides a sound example of the role Curated Fiction can play in complicating the narrative act, in enacting dichotomy and in crafting ambiguity as an agent in and of the narrative act, in this specific instance bringing into the question both the absence of the author and the compelling aesthetic/narrative power of hearing a voice from beyond the grave. Not only do we therefore have a distinct positioning of Jack at the narrative 'centre' of *Last Orders*, lifted out of the consistency of other voices through the unique pattern his verbatim account contains, but we also have a compelling marker of the value of Curated Fiction in celebrating everything that a character's voice can create for the reader and for the architecture of the storyworld: colour, certainly, but also empathy, ambiguity and provocative sources of tension relating to ethical investment in the ever-complicated notion of fictional truth.

Conclusion

Last Orders plays with duality in compelling ways that make provocative use of essentially uncomplicated narrative voices and generates vital aesthetic conversations around presence and absence in the motivation of characters, the layering of personal histories and the importance of connection and community; it shares some similar qualities with *Waterland* in that it utilises a moment in the narrative present to afford its characters the capacity to reflect on what has shaped and defined them. On the surface it is a simple tale of humble men undertaking a compassionate mission, beneath which lies a sophisticated narrative architecture reminding us of the compelling power of trust and ambiguity in the creation of fiction and of the extent to which Curated Fiction can offer multiple aesthetic and narrative choices in facilitating narrative, emotional and moral complexity. In derivations of the speech act and concomitant elements of orality, in allowing characters to both look outwards and within and to trace the influences of the self; these are all made possibilities by the techniques and strategies of Curated Fiction, and in *Last Orders* they generate a narrative fabric of nearly infinite texture.

If the chapters on *Waterland* and *Last Orders* have presented variations on a theme of Curated Fiction, the next chapter will interrogate a novel that comes closest to my conceptual mapping of the term. William Faulkner's *As I Lay Dying* is replicated to some extent in *Last Orders* as I have indicated, but the narrative sweep of Faulkner's novel encompasses such vast narrative and aesthetic domain that it provides a necessary reference point in determining how Curated Fiction can operate as methodology in both the crafting and analysis of fiction. In particular, I will further unpack the notions of polyphony and the extent to which narrative language can work against itself to complicate and enrich a storyworld, and the acts of navigation required to engage/negotiate with it. Ultimately, the ironic notion that an authorial consciousness can be simultaneously present and absent in narrative organisation will be posited as one of the central provocative features of Curated Fiction.

4 Strange Blood

The Anti-Language of *As I Lay Dying*

Context: The Novel

As I Lay Dying (1930) is set in fictional Yoknapatawpha County, based on the area around Oxford, Mississippi where Faulkner was living at the time. Much, if not all, of Faulkner's fiction is set within this regional space; its regionality is clearly inherent in the language and some of the attitudes of his characters. The story concerns the Bundren family (father Anse, sons Darl, Cash, Jewel and Vardaman, and daughter Dewey Dell) and their quest to transport the coffin bearing their deceased wife and mother, Addie, to Jefferson where she wished to be interred—a journey of several days' duration. In all, the novel has sixteen narrators: each member of the family, including Addie post-mortem, has a voice and relates events from their point of view; we also hear from other characters such as Vernon and Cora Tull, their neighbours; the local doctor, Peabody; the Reverend Whitfield; and various other residents and small business owners the Bundrens encounter on their odyssey. As we have seen with *Last Orders* and *Waterland*, the chief central effect of utilising multiple narrative voices is one of authorial absence, as this is an effect embodied and extended in the narrative complexity of *As I Lay Dying*. Similarly, as with the other two novels, it can also be read as a trauma fiction, especially with regard to the accounts of Vardaman, the youngest member of the family who appears to struggle the most with his mother's death; as with both of Graham Swift's novels, there is perhaps a confessional element to this novel as well: narrating as catharsis.

It is briefly worth acknowledging the comparisons that exist between *As I Lay Dying* and *Last Orders*. Aside from the use of multiple homodiegetic narrations, the novels also each feature a chapter consisting of a numbered list, a one-sentence chapter and a chapter narrated post-mortem. The central narrative and thematic shape of both novels is similar; they both concern a journey undertaken for the purpose of conveying the deceased person to their final resting place. It is outside the scope of this book to adjudicate on matters of literary debt or provenance; it is sufficient for me to acknowledge that both novels are richly evocative of their specific times and places through particular oral textures of characters' accounts, which delivers them both into the realm of Curated Fiction.

Curated Fiction and Textures of Voice

As I Lay Dying presents the opportunity to return to one of the essential guiding theories governing the formulation of Curated Fiction, in the work of Mikhail Bakhtin. Polyphony has been explicated in some detail elsewhere, but it should be asserted here that *As I Lay Dying* is also a work clearly underscored by acts of polyphonous utterance. Moreover, according to John Mullan, Bakhtin asserted that disparate voices and the layers of language they codified were capable of eliciting narrative strength: [he] believed that the special power of the Novel as a genre was to assort together "different voices and types of language ... works that make present the clashes and incongruities of different voices were to be preferred to those that create a unified narrative surface" (Mullan 2006, p. 246). If the linguistic texture of Faulkner's novel is anything, it is collisional: voices intersect with varying degrees of fluidity, so that language veers between poetic and functional, mundane and opaque. Of the four novels surveyed for this book, Faulkner's is the most inherently and intrinsically heteroglossic. Alastair Renfrew states that this term (heteroglossia, broadly defined as 'diversity of speech') is "Bakhtin's way of describing the internal condition of any language, its variation and stratification, produced as individual speakers and social groups interact with and against an abstract 'standard' language" (Renfrew 2015, p. 94). Such a theory also informs Bakhtin's ideas regarding novelisation—"how the novel itself is always and definitively in the process of breaking out into other worlds" (94). Theories regarding polyphony have been interrogated and refined in the decades since Bakhtin first formulated them. Caryl Emerson cites Yuri Kriakin doing so, on the basis that polyphony focuses on "verbal dialogue and its current of ideas, tending to ignore the effect of fully embodied scenes" (Emerson 1997, p. 130). Furthermore:

> Bakhtin is wrong ... when he suggests that self-consciousness is the hero of Dostoevsky's novels. Self-deception is the hero—and all of that polyphonic obfuscation, those thought experiments and endless proliferation of alternatives... are designed by their author not to provide the major heroes with invigorating, open-ended options but rather to *thicken and darken the texture of the work* ... and to test the heroes on their conflicted way to the truth.
>
> (ps. 130–1, emphasis added)

This might well have been written directly regarding *As I Lay Dying*. Faulkner's aesthetic approach to the narrative choices he makes are based on 'thickening and darkening'; herein lies the clear appeal of such a technique for Curated Fiction, predicating narration on the basis of simple subjectivity which allows individual narrators to obfuscate and perhaps even experiment with their own telling of stories that other narrators will either endorse, refute, contrast or contradict. It is important to consider polyphony then not as a singular, superficial entity or prism through which the narrative construction of a novel can be perceived; rather, it is a whole-narrative concept, embedded in specific language choices which reveal deeper moral and social complexities—and the ultimate aim of such complexity is to allow characters to dissemble, to either avoid the truth completely or conceal it from themselves for as long as possible. A further criticism of Bakhtin's polyphony is that it precludes 'a silent finger pointing at the truth' (p. 130) which, according to Kriakin, Dostoevsky liked to include in his major scenes. In *As I Lay Dying* we again see vast variation in the function, purpose, intention and shape of language—or, in some cases, the absence of language: Cash is empirical, Anse is self-indulgent, Vardaman is confused, Darl is prophetic, Dewey Dell is naïve. Language in Faulkner's novel is simultaneously useful and brutally ineffective.

Faulkner has composed his assembly of voices so that an interrogation of narrative complexity is invited, if not essential. It affords a clear dissection of the difference between 'who sees and who speaks' (Bal, 1983) and underscoring this is the concept of the disnarrated, "the elements in a narrative that explicitly consider and refer to what does not take place" (Prince 2003, p. 22). I will contend that Vardaman provides examples of this in the novel and that the disnarrated can provide yet another arrow in the quiver of Curated Fiction. *As I Lay Dying* also invites reading as a regret narrative (Beatty, 2017), by which we can dissect alternative points of departure for events in the novel and work backwards from them to entertain different narrative possibilities and how characters might have responded differently had different choices been made. Regret narratives offer close alignment with the principles of Curated Fiction and work to create narrative richness; if a compelling development of fictional possibility is generated by the author asking 'What if?', regret narratives also afford the reader this opportunity. For these reasons, *As I Lay Dying* allows further close examination of Curated Fiction in practice. The novel inhabits a self-contained linguistic universe which not only locates it regionally; Faulkner institutes polyphony to inhabit the minds and perceptions of his characters to create a network of associations, connections, responses and provocations within and between each of the novel's accounts. I will subsequently interrogate the intersection between orality and narration to enact variability of narrative roles between characters; Darl is imbued with powers of omniscience and many characters with degrees of unreliability. I will offer analyses of the characters of Darl and Vardaman as exemplars of a triangular, polyphonous character-narration-language construct; I will also examine Addie's narration as further illustrating the merits of narrating postmortem in the context of Curated Fiction. In particular I will argue that despite his descent into madness, it is Darl who acts essentially as a Curator (delineating Faulkner's authorial absence from the narrative project), coalescing his powers of omniscience to provide commentary beyond his immediate or knowable experience within the storyworld of this novel; indeed, there may be some correlation between his omniscience and his apparent departure from sanity at the novel's conclusion.

Curated Fiction and 'Filling a Lack'

Curated Fiction as a narrative construct draws on the evolution of techniques such as stream-of-consciousness and second-person narration. Faulkner's propensity to experiment with narrative form and voice may have emanated directly from the impetus of modernist writers to completely reinvent language and through that reinvention, reshape the way the world is represented. As with *Waterland*, we will come to identify *As I Lay Dying* as an explicitly polyphonous work; explicitly, because Faulkner offers acute constructions of language that are intended to illuminate thought-processes as well as inhabit character, drive the action, offer reflection and (as mentioned) create ambiguity. Judith Lockyer notes that "Addie is the novel's strongest proponent of the frailty of language, [and] Darl Bundren embodies the conviction that the word can create reality and connect isolated consciousnesses" (Lockyer 1987, 165); perceptions and tensions that exist in the narrative space between these apparently contrasting positions are enacted by curation. Specifically, we can perceive Curated Fiction as narratively holistic; if someone's account of a specific event (their experience and their perception of it) is definitive, it is so because language has created definition—arguably, this is Darl's main function. Similarly, if someone wants to dissemble, or distort an account of something, language offers the opportunity to do so—indeed, words become "a shape to fill a lack" to use Addie's memorable phrase (*As I Lay Dying*, p. 156). In other words, acts of curation can occur at the individual level as well as the macro level, the organisational level, and the two positions Addie and Darl occupy along Faulkner's narrative spectrum provide sound illustration of this.

In Faulkner's willingness to experiment, we find evidence of a novelist using the vernacular and social stratification inherent in his local regionality to inhabit a modernist literary world. *As I Lay Dying* works as multiple meeting points: 'simple' working-class folk, undertaking the apparently mundane task of observing their wife/mother's wish to be buried with her own folk, ferrying her body in its handcrafted coffin across a landscape symbolised through fire and flood, rendered in language that is simultaneously poetic, melancholic, absurd and deceptively simplistic—and more importantly, language that is explicitly identified as being restrictive in its capacity for narration, as we note Addie's complaint that "words don't ever fit what they are trying to say at" (*As I Lay Dying*, p. 155). For these reasons, *As I Lay Dying* provides specific insight into the core narrative and aesthetic function of Curated Fiction, namely that a direct sense of navigation is required by the reader to orient themselves within the storyworld in order to process what is happening and why, and also that language and perspective are manipulated through multiple points of view to complicate perceptions of events and how characters (and by extension the reader) may respond to them. It should be noted that in crafting this approach, Faulkner pretends at omniscience; *As I Lay Dying* is Curated Fiction without an (immediately) apparent Curator. Such absence is another agent in the 'thickening and darkening' of the storyworld and the experience of engaging with it; the tension inherent in doing so is what underscores the power of Curated Fiction as narrative architecture. I will return to the notion of Faulkner's absence later in this chapter, but first I will explicate the concept of "regret narratives" (Beatty 2017) as another means by which Faulkner thickens and darkens his novel.

Curated Fiction and the Disnarrated: Regret Narratives and Implied Authorship

Regret narratives can elicit a sense of unreliable narration, another component of Curated Fiction. In his paper *Narrative Possibility and Narrative Explanation*, John Beatty uses a diagram, such as below, to illustrate "the structure of the world described and explained by narratives" (2017, p. 31).

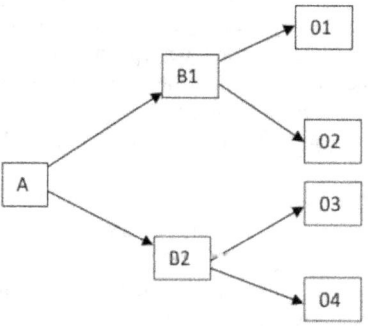

Beatty contends that:

> A—B1—02 explains 02 in the context of surrounding branches. Such a narrative is a causal explanation in the sense that it highlights counterfactual difference-making events. But it is a particular kind of counterfactual difference-making explanation … The unrealised histories A—B2—03 and A—B2—04 are relevant context. They communicate that B1 was not bound to occur at the time of A, B2 was also a real possibility and that 02 would not have occurred had B2 occurred instead.
>
> (ps. 31–2)

Narrative possibility is governed by choice: choices made by authors, experienced/enacted by characters. In addition, such a diagram might be connected to structural choice, in terms of a sequence of events; the author might begin with O4 and conclude at B1, for example, working backwards from a concluding episode to navigate the events that created it and/or explore some of the choices made and the consequences they triggered. Among other things, this also affords the utility of time as a governing structural principle. Beatty further argues that regret narratives "will hopefully motivate close attention to ways in which they help us make sense of things ... it involves comparing what happened with what in fact did not" (32–3). We only have regret that we did not follow a different path or make a different choice.

The utility of this approach for Curated Fiction is considerable. The Curator is, for argument's sake, positioned at A while the array of narrators are at O1, O2, O3 and so on; the narrators may or may not express regret at their involvement in the events being narrated but it is entirely possible for the Curator to do so. This affords the Curator a role that might be recognised as judgemental—especially if the Curator offers some subjective or intrusive commentary on the events of the story. Thus, a complexity of relationships is possible: the Curator might regard Narrator O2 fondly but distrust O1, be related to O4 but in love with O3, and so on. This may determine who is privileged or marginalised in the construction (telling) of the story—and it delineates one narrative while recognising, which the reader may also recognise, that others are possible. With reference to Curated Fiction, regret narratives should be linked to the Implied Author, and for context I will briefly revisit some notions relating to aesthetic distance. According to Booth, "the novelist will find himself in difficulties if he tries to discover some ideal distance that all works ought to seek" (2003, p. 123). To summarise, if distance in a work is too great, the work may disconnect the reader as being improbable or absurd; if too close, "the work becomes too personal and cannot be enjoyed as art" (p. 122). Booth continues,

> 'Aesthetic distance' is in fact many different effects, some of them quite inappropriate to some kinds of works. More important, distance is never an end in itself ... When Chikamatsu, for example, urges that poets avoid all emotional epithets, he does so in order to increase the emotional effect in the reader. ... "It is essential that one not say of a thing that 'it is sad', but that it be sad of itself." When Brecht ... asks for a 'pervading coolness' ... what he really wants is to increase the emotional distance in order to involve the reader's social judgement more deeply.
>
> (p. 123)

In *As I Lay Dying*, Dewey Dell encapsulates the features of a regret narrative; through this lens, we can also determine Faulkner's nebulous presence as an Implied Author. Dewey Dell does not reveal her pregnancy to anyone in her family (although Darl knows) and resolves to procure an abortion when the family arrives in Jackson for Addie's interment; this brings her into contact with a shady drug store owner named MacGowan, who takes advantage of her. In return for the promise of a successful treatment, he lures Dewey Dell into a sexual encounter; to compound matters, the money to pay for the abortion is stolen by Anse. Dewey Dell realises she has been fooled by MacGowan: "She looks at me [Vardaman]. 'It ain't going to work', she says. 'That son of a bitch'". (*As I Lay Dying*, p. 232). She states 'it ain't going to work' several times, clearly grappling with the enormity of this fact in her mind. One of Faulkner's gifts is the ability to create empathy for his characters; arguably, Dewey Dell even has a sort of comic nobility about her. This is crushed in the next section of the novel she narrates, as Anse interrogates her about the source of the money he takes from her, and she is reduced to a series of exasperated pleas: "Pa. Pa. ... It was give to me. To buy something with. ... Pa. Pa." (p. 236) Dewey Dell's arc in the story represents a regret narrative in that, despite her efforts, she will remain pregnant. There is mounting tension between her and Darl over the pregnancy as he refuses to take action either against Lafe, the father of the child, or by telling Anse. She attacks Darl near the end of the novel, "scratching and clawing at him like a wild cat" (p. 218); perhaps, if we read her arc as a regret narrative, this is catharsis, the moment of frustrations being released as Dewey Dell confronts the futility of her actions. She rarely makes distinct emotional declarations, so attacking Darl, venting her frustration at her failure to procure an abortion, is an intense dramatic moment. However, she is stoic throughout the novel as many of the characters are; this compounds the tragedy of their circumstances. We, as Readers, are invited to fill in some emotional gaps. Such gaps are nearly essential in the construction of Curated Fiction and therefore regret narratives and resulting emotional distance are central features of this framework. Implied authorship, then, must have an 'implied reader'; the success of a work of fiction may depend on the successful navigation of it by that reader. In other words, the more obtuse or 'difficult' a work, the more sophisticated the act of navigation must be. Booth argues that

> ...though the old-style effort to find the theme or moral has been generally repudiated, the new-style search for the 'meaning' which the work 'communicates' or 'symbolises' can yield the same kinds of misreading. ... Both types of search ... express a basic need: the reader's need to know where, in the world of values, he stands—that is, to know where the author wants him to stand.
>
> (Booth 2003, p. 73)

Booth further argues that the complexity of works of fiction is such that to identify any one meaning and "to announce it as what the work is for is to do a very small part of the critical task" (73); more significantly, "writers who are successful in getting their readers to reserve judgement are not impartial about whether judgement should be reserved" (p. 77). This allows us to converse, as it were, with Faulkner: are we to judge Dewey Dell for her pregnancy? Are we to judge Anse for his laziness and opportunism? Vardaman for drilling holes into his deceased mother's face? Darl for setting the barn on fire? These are complex questions, and different readers will answer them differently; the answers may be complicated and are not necessarily the focus of this book, however it is worth considering the variability with which Faulkner invites such judgement.

To what extent then can it be argued that Faulkner is absent from this work? That there is no clear answer to such a question illustrates the value of Curated Fiction as an aesthetic principle, one which uncouples a story from the circumstance of its creation or the identity of its author. On first appearance, Faulkner seems absent as there no evidence of his direct narrative intrusion into the novel's events; however, we can assume that the chapters as they appear in the book are arranged in their order for specific reasons, suggesting a sense of coordination that we identify as authorial; in addition, and with considerable sophistication, the subtle ways in which readers are invited to judge characters provides evidence of Faulkner 'watching' us read.

Gerald Prince coins the term "disnarrated" which provides another frame for this discussion about the intersection between author/narrator/character/reader (Prince 1988); essentially, the disnarrated represents "the paradox of 'narrating' or including in a narrative what does not occur" (Beatty 2017, p. 35). The disnarrated might include

> Unfulfilled expectations, unwarranted beliefs, failed attempts, crushed hopes, suppositions and false calculations, errors and lies, and so forth ... the disnarrated provides one of the important means for *emphasising tellability*, this narrative is worth narrating because it could not have been otherwise, because it usually is otherwise, because it was not otherwise.
>
> (Prince 1988, p. 5, emphasis added)

'Tellability' is key here, recalling the tension between diegesis and mimesis in fundamental considerations of narrative voice. In addition, concepts of orality are also returned to focus—Faulkner is not narrating *As I Lay Dying*, he is telling it (through, of course, the multiple voices of his characters—so perhaps more accurately, they are telling it). Dewey Dell epitomises the failed attempts and crushed hopes about which Prince writes; consequently, 'simultaneous' narration is occurring, and the reader might reasonably ask, 'What if she had been successful?' In terms of dramatic irony, perhaps the reader understands that she will not be; she might have been; it may make no difference to her family, since Addie is still dead and requires burial and this is the overriding narrative situation of the novel. Since it is not terminated, however, her pregnancy may make a difference to the family after the events of the novel have concluded. On this basis, it is possible to dissect and examine narrative layers that are composed of hypothetical or counterfactual events as much as they are actual, narrated events, and as such, the disnarrated is a valid source of narrative enrichment in the context of Curated Fiction, whereby the subjectivity of narrative accounts will lead to possible omissions, contradictions, gaps, misunderstandings or assumptions. Tension therefore exists within the curatorial role, emanating from the extent to which these matters should be 'tidied up' or not in the act of curation.

Curated Fiction and Unreliable Truth: Vardaman and Addie

Constant navigation is required in engaging with the various narrative threads of *As I Lay Dying*, owing to the aesthetic choices Faulkner has made in employing sixteen different narrators and maintaining authorial distance. One specific effect of this consequence is a deliberate confusion; as Booth says, "Many modern works use the same kind of confusing, unreliable narration in a deliberate polemic against the conventional notions of reality and in favour of the superior reality given by the world of the book" (2003, p. 288). Such an effect fits inside a broader discussion that embeds narrative unreliability within Curated Fiction. P.K. Hansen defines unreliable narration as occurring when the act of reading "changes focus from what is being told to the one who is telling" (2007, p. 230). This is likely to inculcate subjectivity; significantly, it precludes authorial presence. Faulkner himself has claimed that "tragedy is the impossibility—or at least the tremendous difficulty, of communication" (Meriwether & Millgate 1980, ps. 70–1). Curated Fiction, then, can be delineated as a sequence of acts confronting that impossibility. If experience of an event is subjective, Curated Fiction privileges the experience rather than the event and in doing so, communicates character as an inherent factor within the narrative act.

To illustrate this point, I will focus on the character of Vardaman, before offering an examination of Addie's chapter and the role of Darl. In differing ways, Vardaman and Darl both embody this concept in the novel, but I will discuss Darl subsequently in relation to omniscience, to evince the argument that he is the novel's Curator. Like Darl, Vardaman has a unique and specific language frame in the novel; he is approximately ten years old (his exact age is never specified) and struggling to process the events he witnesses, most significantly of course the death of his mother. According to Kathryn Olsen, "Vardaman's understanding of the world and his unique way of expressing it are crucial to this novel" (2010, p. 104). This is evident in two incidents: his single-sentence chapter, 'My mother is a fish' (*As I Lay Dying*, p. 73), and the episode in which—thinking that his mother cannot breathe inside her coffin, itself a touching reminder that he is not aware of the truth—he drills holes in the lid, consequently injuring his mother's face. Both of these represent different facets of unreliability as a narrative construct; the former, as a statement of metaphor, precludes the clear truth of Addie Bundren's human form, and the second presents a grotesque fact that threatens to intrude on reader engagement—it may, however briefly, shock us out of the story. Prior to seeing his mother die, Vardaman has caught a fish which is cut up into pieces of 'not-fish' so that Vardaman has 'not-blood' on his hands (p. 47). Vardaman's narration is perhaps the most explicitly confusing of any of the novel's voices; he is almost constantly conflating images and experiences, many of them with the state of his mother. He is alarmed that Cash intends to secure her in the coffin he has made: "I said, are you going to nail it shut Cash. Nail it? Nail it?" (p. 58). On the following page, Vardaman appears to have confused his mother with both a rabbit and the not-fish:

> and so if Cash nails the box up, she is not a rabbit. And so if she is not a rabbit I couldn't breathe in the crib and Cash is going to nail it up. And so if she lets him it is not her. I know. I was there. I saw when it did not be her. I saw. They think it is and Cash is going to nail it up. It was not her because it was lying right yonder in the dirt. And now it's all chopped up. I chopped it up. It's laying in the kitchen in the bleeding pan.
>
> (59)

Vardaman is attempting to process his experiences, and of interest here is how the narrative act of processing is rendered. Much of Vardaman's narration is almost but not quite stream-of-consciousness, where essentially normal editorial conventions regarding punctuation and the sequencing of thoughts has been removed. Additionally, as Olsen states,

> [Vardaman] manipulates language in the most overt manner, purging his mother's death by identifying her with the fish he catches and subsequently dismembers. He does more than simply conflate the two deaths, though. Rather, Vardaman uses negation and annihilation, unraveling the functions of language in time and space, to spur the regeneration of his mother as an active force.
>
> (2010, p. 104)

Echoed in the novel extract quoted above are two notions that are clearly dominant in his thinking: that is mother is not in the coffin, and that Cash is going to nail it up. His drilling 'breathing holes' in the lid of the coffin, which unintentionally damages her face, is a poignant yet confronting demonstration of both his innocence and dramatic irony; we, as Readers, know that she is deceased.

Through the lens of Curated Fiction, Vardaman's role in the narrative project of *As I Lay Dying* is compelling. The specific semantics of his narrative voice illustrate the concept that, in Curated Fiction, voice can equal character. If we consider that Curated Fiction allows for the stratification of meaning within and between narrative voices, that meaning will be derived from multiple sources, and specifically individual, idiosyncratic perceptions of particular events—in this case, Addie's death and her desire to be buried in Jefferson—is the most abundant source. Through Vardaman, the nature of reality in Faulkner's storyworld is questioned, literature has little fundamental purpose if not to pose significant questions about the intersection between truth and fiction and the shifting relationship that authors, narrators, characters and readers might exhibit with it. Curated Fiction enacts an ironic inadequacy of language.

Addie Bundren's chapter perfectly encapsulates Faulkner's "impossibility of communication", most explicitly in her claim "That was when I learned that words are no good; that words don't ever fit what they are trying to say at" (*As I Lay Dying*, p. 155). Addie's chapter centralises the idea that Faulkner is not, in this novel, advocating language merely as a means of communication—indeed, the notion seems nearly trivial. Rather, he replaces language with self: the characters of this novel are embodiments of language, and thus of narration. He is able to do this because of the pluralised opportunity that Curated Fiction affords, to divide perception across a variety of characters who are each attempting to maintain their sense of self in increasingly fraught emotional circumstances. Bleikasten asserts that "selves are fictions anyhow—more or less random, more or less ingenious combinations of images and identifications. Selves are texts: motely tissues woven from reminiscences and borrowings: the pattern may be new and original, the material never is" (1990, p. 3). Perhaps *As I Lay Dying* can be read as a sequence of dissolving selves; Dewey Dell loses her composure at the end of the novel, arguably in light of her failure to procure an abortion; Darl's sanity unravels; Cash's dissolution is physical, in the form of his broken leg; Addie literally decomposes. P.K. Babu reminds us that "in Faulkner the persistence of the writerly dilemma of constituting a narrated self while relying on an ever elusive medium of language, is cogent" (2016, p. 18). This dissolution of the self is possible via Curated Fiction in that a Curator is allowing characters to speak for themselves; as a result, characters will make decisions about what is revealed and what is concealed and consequently they will reveal something of themselves—as trustworthy or not, for example. This might be considered a sense of narrative (dis)honesty—when given the opportunity to record events in which you played a significant part, and your role in those events was not (for whatever reason) admirable, to what extent do you rewrite that role? This also feeds into considerations of unreliable narration—however, I don't consider Addie's narration unreliable; her account is rather one of 'setting the record straight' and even filling in gaps that have emerged in our comprehension of the story to that point: identifying Jewel's father, for example, as the Reverend Whitfield.

Addie's section enacts, to use the phrase from this chapter's title, anti-language. This is evident physically in the text:

> ...and then I would find that I had forgotten the name of the jar. I would think: the shape of my body where I used to be a virgin is the shape of a   and I couldn't think *Anse,* couldn't remember *Anse*. It was not that I could think of myself as no longer unvirgin, because I was three now.
>
> (As I Lay Dying, p. 157)

The physical gap signifies thought entering the text: Addie does not have a word to describe the shape she needs—this is literally, to paraphrase another of Addie's aphorisms, the lack standing in for the shape (of the word). Kaufman argues that the gap is "an inverse of the coffin. Addie's womb instead of her tomb, a lack instead of a presence" (1993, p. 113). Gaps permeate the novel in varied ways, perhaps most notably within narrations as some characters (Vardaman, as we have seen, and Darl) struggle to connect events with experience, or the actions of family members with common sense. Gaps also occur between narrative events; it is significant that Darl narrates the moment of Addie's death despite not being present at the house to witness it. One thematic through-line of the novel presents the Bundrens as a fractured family unit and Addie confirms this by ruminating how words, with their gaps between meaning and intention, are nearly always the cause of such fracturing. Faulkner weaves a clever oxymoronic thread through the novel: as Kaufman concisely summarises, "Opposites equal, absence makes presence" (p. 113).

Addie's voice renders the novel unreal: the impact of this in a work that is already freely innovating narrative methods, voices and structures cannot be underestimated. Curated Fiction, then, allows for some profound ironies to be facilitated in creating fiction: the perception of an experience can become the experience, and the recounting of an event can become the event. Importantly, as a result, the line between character and narration blurs, and with it the traditional demarcations that separate truth, reality, and fiction. In this way, language can be made to work against itself, to reveal meaning through what it cannot, or is not allowed to, convey.

Curated Fiction and Omniscience: Darl as Curator

As noted, Darl narrates the moment of Addie's death (which he perceives, not being present when it happens). I will now examine Darl's role in the novel as a Curator, and in doing so I will first consider the concept of a narrator's isolation. According to Booth:

> Perhaps the most important effect of traveling with a narrator who is unaccompanied by a helpful author is that of decreasing emotional distance. We

have seen that much traditional commentary was used to increase sympathy or to apologise for faults. When an author chooses to forego such rhetoric, he may do so because ... his central intelligence is of the kind that will seem most sympathetic if presented as an isolated, unaided consciousness, without the support that a reliable narrator or observer would lend. ...So long as what the character thinks and feels can be taken directly as a reliable clue about the circumstances he faces, the reader can experience those circumstances with him even more strongly because of his moral isolation. Such isolation can be used to create an almost unbearably poignant sense of the hero's or heroine's helplessness in a chaotic, friendless world.

(*Rhetoric of Fiction*, p. 274)

Darl is arguably the privileged narrator of the novel, and this alone imbues him with some Curatorial qualities. He narrates most frequently and seems to have powers not afforded other characters—namely, to narrate the thoughts of others, as well as narrating events at which he is not present. He and Vardaman represent either end of the narrative spectrum of the novel; Vardaman appears naïve and unable to process the events in which he is involved; Darl, on the other hand, not only processes what is happening but is actively involved in much of it, directly or presumptively. Questions of reliability concerning the novel's narrations coalesce around him: he seems to walk a tenuous line between a structural role (narrator as mediator) and a semantic role, or narrator as character (Hansen 2007, 231). With specific reference to concepts of Curated Fiction, it is through Darl that conditions of ambiguity enter the novel; in this case, the reader must navigate the ending with specific regard to whether or not Darl descends into insanity. His breakdown can be read as a dramatic manifestation of the novel's core tension, between speaking/acting and meaning: a significant irony, for example, exists in the fact that it is Darl who attempts to burn down the barn where Addie's coffin is stored at the end of a day's travel (and not so long after Darl has been instrumental in saving the coffin after it was washed off their wagon during a courageous but poorly planned attempt to cross a flooded river). The irony is twofold; Darl reports that "I cannot love my mother because I have no mother" (*As I Lay Dying*, p. 82) and later on, Cash rationalises Darl's actions in setting the fire: "and then when Darl seen that it looked like one of us would have to do something, I can also believe he done right in a way" (*As I Lay Dying*, p. 214). It is the setting of the fire that prompts the family to consider Darl insane; however, reaction to the arson attack also allows Faulkner to further illustrate Anse as someone willing to take any shortcuts and save money by any means necessary, as it is easier to have Darl committed to an asylum than to face a lawsuit for the loss of the barn. Darl disowns his mother, and is in turn disowned by Addie in her chapter, so there is little of a meaningful maternal relationship in place—and yet it is Darl, in setting fire to the barn, who acts to conclusively end the ordeal of the family's funeral procession and commit his mother to ashes. He does not succeed; Jewel burns himself badly in recovering the coffin from the flames. The setting of the fire, however, affords Darl a controlling hand in the narrative, essential in recognising Darl as Curator. This is subsequently complicated by the representation of his insanity, the ambiguous realisation of which compounds the entanglement of reader/storyworld trust and establishes yet again the crucial element of unreliability.

I contend that this further distances the author from the act/s of narration. We recognise a triangular relationship at work in the reading of a novel—between the reader, the narrator(s) and the author. On some occasions the author and the narrator may be the same person; on other occasions, the author imparts responsibilities for narration onto one or more of his or her characters—but in doing so there remains vestiges of authorial presence in the ordering of chapters or decisions regarding sequence and so on. This reinforces the important notion that authorial absence in a work of fiction can only ever be an illusion (Booth, 1983), however comprehensive and well-conceived the illusion might be. In *As I Lay Dying*, Faulkner exposes the reader to a complex game of shifting roles, cross-referencing, and varying perceptions—and in doing so, provocatively situates language itself as being insufficient. This is most clearly evident in the chapter narrated by Addie Bundren herself who, when she 'speaks' in the novel, has been dead for three or four days but it is equally present in the shift away from reality that Darl experiences as the novel progresses. Significantly though, Faulkner establishes and maintains tension in that gap between how words are used and what they mean—a tension that Michael Kaufmann summarises as "narrative [that] reflects the fossilizing print that embodies it, a shaping force but also an encasing one" (1993, 101). Thus, in Darl, as with Addie and Vardaman, we have a representation of language acting in contrast with its function to tell; this is the central, elemental tension at the heart of Curated Fiction and its propensity to enrich narrative texture.

Conclusion

As I Lay Dying can be mapped using Curated Fiction as a guiding principle, whereby subjectivity and truth in the telling can be undermined by inherent self-interest, naivety or self-consciousness on the part of respective individual narrators; by the devolution of language to self; by the propensity for language to be contradictory or absence-making as much as it can distil or clarify. The result is a negotiable junction at which author, narrator, character, and reader come together to navigate the various experiences such a project affords. This extends our understanding of fiction and its possibilities well beyond what Mikhail Bakhtin believed was "works that make present the clashes and incongruities of different voices" (Mullan 2006, 246); those clashes and incongruities extend from voice outwards into the realm of perception and consequent emotional truths. In Curated Fiction, these points of intersection—where language meets and must deal with its absence, where self meets experience—are made explicit so that a meaningful and/or provocative engagement with the storyworld and its many invitations is catalysed. In the next chapter, I will explore a work in which intentions of the author are rendered explicit, undermining—negating, even—the important illusion on which Curated Fiction relies.

5 The Secret Room

Artifice and Historical Angst in *A Room Made of Leaves*

Context: The Novel

Kate Grenville's *A Room Made of Leaves* was published in 2020 and is essentially an imagined autobiography of Elizabeth Macarthur, who played a prominent role in the very early colonial settlement of Australia. The central narrative device of the novel is that Macarthur kept an ostensibly secret journal which Grenville has uncovered, in circumstances that are explicated in an 'Editor's Note' (at the beginning of the novel) and an 'Author's Note' (at its conclusion). In between these Notes we are treated to a masterful unfolding of historical detail—so much so, that we might be left "wondering whether there is any fiction in it at all" (Garvey, 2022 p. 214). This interplay between historical fact and the writing of fiction is worth examining through the prism of Curated Fiction, certainly, and this chapter will undertake some analysis of that aspect of the novel; of more significant interest, however, is the novel's aforementioned framing device, the two 'Notes', which establish the premise by which the content of the novel came to be discovered and then reveal that premise as, itself, a fiction. I will argue that since Grenville has drawn back the curtain of narrative artifice to reveal her sleight of hand, *A Room Made of Leaves* cannot be considered a true work of Curated Fiction—not in the way that the previous novels in this book have been situated, all of which either sustain the artifice (*Last Orders*) or have no semblance of artifice at all (*Waterland* and *As I Lay Dying*). In other words, I would like to strengthen conceptual understandings of Curated Fiction by illustrating a contradictory example—of what Curated Fiction, essentially, is not. For the purposes of this illustration I will position *A Room Made of Leaves* as an act of artful deception, and discuss this provocative term with specific regard to its value and function within the craft of novel-writing.

There are several sources of context through which we can examine Grenville's construction of her novel, and while not all of them are strictly relevant to my purposes for this argument they are worthy of consideration in the wider discussion about the ethics of fiction and its interplay with trust and truth. Perhaps most importantly, *A Room Made of Leaves* is situated firmly

DOI: 10.4324/9781032635477-5

within in the genre of historical fiction; on this basis alone it is easy to deduce that Grenville should be concerned with some degree of veracity regarding her subject matter. However, Grenville is no stranger when it comes to controversy over her occupation of that shadowy domain between history and fiction; her award-winning earlier novel, *The Secret River* (2005), incited considerable debate over the writing of Australian colonial history and the extent to which lines between historical fact and fictional truth had been blurred. *The Secret River* tells the story of the Thornhill family headed by William, an emancipated convict, who has been awarded a parcel of land on the Hawkesbury River with his freedom. He finds, on arrival, that the land is occupied by a Dharug family, whose ancestors have lived on and cared for the land for tens of thousands of years. Contact between the two families results in the brutal massacre of the latter, and thus the violent and confronting nature of the colonisation of Australia is examined in microcosm. The novel speaks clearly into a narrative of Australia's recent past that might be termed 'violence and then silence'; historians such Professor W.H. Stanner coined the term 'the Great Australian Silence' whereby such acts of violent dispossession have been ignored or, at the very least, marginalised in our national conversation. *The Secret River* therefore was Kate Grenville's attempt to 'retell our stories and put the shadows in' (Grenville, 2005).

A Room Made of Leaves and Historical Truth

This affords an opportunity to briefly examine the intersection between fiction, truth and history. While I would love to provide some philosophical context that delineates the relationship between fact and truth, I fear that such a discussion would derail the broader purpose of this book, which is to explicate one particular methodology of novel writing; however, since that methodology incorporates the extent to which fiction must create truth, some definitions are perhaps necessary. For the purposes of this analysis, something defined as fact must have the weight of objective empirical being, whereas something that is defined as truth can include elements of subjective experience. In this manner, concepts of truth allow for interpretations of events that occurred which may differ according to perception and the frailty of memory. For example, it is a fact that the Australian Constitution came into effect on January 1, 1901 and that the period of our history known as Federation commences from that date. A contemporary interpretation of the Constitution—a truth regarding that document, according to some perspectives—is that it failed to acknowledge the presence in Australia of its First Nations and is therefore, to some extent, racist. (A referendum to change the Constitution allowing the federal Australian government to make laws in respect of the First Nations people of this country was held in 1967 and was successful.) To a profound extent, the colonial and post-colonial history of Australia as a settler nation has become politicised; former Prime Minister John Howard railed against what he termed the 'black arm band view' of history, and during his term in office (1996–2007) he refused to issue an Apology to the generations of aboriginal children taken from their families, sometimes forcefully, as part of government policies of assimilation during the middle decades of the twentieth century. His successor, Kevin Rudd—from the opposing end of the political spectrum—issued such an Apology as one his first Prime Ministerial acts, in February 2008.

In part, Howard's terminology also captured the extent to which we might feel guilt or shame for the violence and dispossession that occurred following 1788, when the First Fleet arrived in what is now Sydney Harbour. There are accounts of violent conflicts between settlers and Aboriginal people, some of which could fairly be described as massacres of the latter; in Tasmania, where I live, the process of trying to eliminate indigenous people from their land can fairly be described as attempted genocide; where they couldn't be killed, they were rounded up, dislocated from their country and housed in settlements where they could conveniently be forgotten[1]. Conservative historians have attempted to revise such histories, downplaying the violence and offering a rather selective interpretation of sources in order to present an alternative view of events; it is into this debate, about the apparently subjective veracity of history and its capacity to define us in contemporary times, that Kate Grenville wrote *The Secret River.*

According to Inga Clendinnen, in her magisterial Quarterly Essay *The History Question: Who Owns the Past?*, we should approach the 'history' of Grenville's novel with some trepidation; Grenville seems to have operated, in writing this novel, on the assumption that "history is, or ought to be, about finding and telling stories...Grenville sees her novel as a work of history sailing triumphantly beyond the constrictions of the formal discipline of history-writing" (Clendinnen, 2006, p. 17) The clear inference is that *The Secret River* as a work of fiction also wants to sit with readers as a work of history—that Grenville's mission, in part, was to put the 'story' back into history. However, the controversy lies in 'sailing triumphantly beyond' the conventions of writing history in order to craft a work of fiction; arguably, the two conventions might seem incompatible, given that the writing of history (properly pursued) is a quest for knowledge informed as far as possible by the ascertainment of empirical fact. Elsewhere in her essay, Clendinnen identifies the limitations of writing history—reproducing daily conversations is not possible, for example, and nor is having access to a historical figure's 'inner monologue'—what someone was thinking or feeling on a particular day in particular circumstances can never be accurately determined. The genre known as 'historical fiction' is defined, arguably, by works in which historical events are overlaid with invented characters and situations; importantly, the empirical facts of such events may be adapted to help establish the fictional storyworld. Such adaptation precludes the work from being considered a reliable historical record. *The Secret River*, then, occupies a contested space: historians may take exceptions to its historical pretentions, while novelists will generally defend Grenville's right to invention and artifice.

For the purposes of this chapter, I regard *A Room Made of Leaves* as a response of sorts to *The Secret River* and its attendant debates. Fundamentally, Grenville has sought to clearly establish the parameters of invention for *A Room Made of Leaves* and therefore remove any notion of her work being contested; however, difficulty remains in her dealing with a historical figure and recreating the details of that figure's life from an entirely subjective point of view. It is within these parameters of invention that we can identify the source of artful deception mentioned earlier, which I will unpack further in due course. By establishing such parameters, Grenville has waded into some complex ethical terrain, in providing her fictionalised Elizabeth Macarthur with contemporary sensibilities regarding Aboriginal people. Grenville's device is that Macarthur is writing her memoirs towards the end of her life, looking back on her first years in the colony; according to Charlotte Guest:

> ...even if we allow the voice of the younger, more conciliatory Elizabeth to preside over the older version supposedly penning her memoir, Grenville endows Elizabeth with a level of deference to and respect for Aboriginal people, land and culture that her letters prove not to be the case. For Grenville to superimpose her own politics onto that of her protagonist ultimately does a disservice to history as it presents…a colonist…in a too-favourable light.
>
> (Guest, 2020, p. 213)

Let us revisit Umberto Eco's exploration of the notions of trust and truth, explored in *Six Walks in the Fictional Woods*, in order to unpack this element of Grenville's novel:

> We believe that, so far as the actual world is concerned, truth is the most important criterion, whereas we tend to think that fiction describes a world we have to take as it is, on trust. Even in the actual world, however, the principle of trust is as important as the principle of truth.
>
> (Eco, 1994, p. 89)

When presented with a statement—'It's cold outside', for example—we have a choice: can believe this statement perhaps because we trust the ability of the person who made it to assess and accurately report the temperature; or we can silently question the veracity of this statement and either duck outside to see for ourselves, or gauge our own understanding of the temperature; doing so might require that we accept physiological variations in how individual people 'feel the cold'. In other words, we can accept the statement on trust, or we can determine for ourselves whether or not it's true. Broadly, a work of fiction requests that we take the storyworld and characters within that work on trust: that we rely on the creator of that storyworld and those characters to convince us that what happens there, to those characters, is valid and/or believable. This concept is complicated when it comes to the writing of historical fiction, because the writer is starting with a character or events that have existed or occurred, and for which any number of records and documents might exist that provide (hopefully) reliable accounts that encapsulate that existence or those occurrences; therefore, a contract of trust is arguably established *before* the reader comes to the story. If, in writing historical fiction, the writer makes use of that much-maligned tool known as 'artistic licence', the fictional representation of the actual events or characters may be distorted. In *The Secret River*, Grenville neatly stepped around this by casting that novel with completely invented characters; ironically, in *A Room Made of Leaves*, she clearly establishes her presentation of a real person as fiction. In doing so, she deliciously complicates the interface between history and fiction; a similar case might be made for Quentin Tarantino's film *Inglourious Basterds* which gleefully and bombastically rewrites the ending of World War Two.

However, while Grenville has clearly made some specific aesthetic decisions in the crafting and framing of her novel—decisions which could easily be construed as acts of curation—why isn't the novel an example of Curated Fiction?

Revealing the Trick

A Room Made of Leaves has as its epigraph the phrase, 'Do not believe too quickly!', attributed to Elizabeth Macarthur (although almost certainly the quote is made up). In Chapter 1, I note that central to the concept of Curated Fiction is the illusion of authorial invisibility. It is worth placing the novel in a theoretical context from which it is then possible to extrapolate some threads of narrative design that Grenville has chosen to weave through her novel; in summary, it is possible that consider that *A Room Made of Leaves* provides a sort of literary equivalent of the famous 'Schrödinger's Cat' thought experiment; apparently, Grenville wishes to be both present and absent from her novel at the same time. Because of this duality, and in light of the framing device by which it is present in the work, I would disqualify *A Room Made of Leaves* as a work of Curated Fiction; only when the illusion of authorial absence is sustained, can we begin to consider that a work exemplifies this model.

However, the novel is worthy of discussion and analysis for the opportunities it affords in dissecting some fundamental mechanics of how fiction works. In his essay 'The Structure of Narrative Transmission' (1972), Seymour Chatman unpacks some essential qualities of narrative and story. It might be rather a cliché to mention that good writing is the difference between showing and telling; these principles have evolved from the time of Aristotle and have formed the basis (with significant additions of complexity) of modern narratology. As I have already established, we can consider that with regard to writing fiction, there can be no 'showing' (mimesis), but only forms and methods of telling (diegesis); perhaps 'showing' lends itself more to theatre or cinema. Chatman notes, however, that:

> a certain posture in the ballet, a series of film shots, a whole paragraph in a novel, or only a single word—any of these might be the actualisation of a single narrative statement, since *narrative* as such is independent of medium.
>
> (2004, p. 97; italics in the original.)

A more accurate interpretation of the concept of 'showing and telling' might be found in considering the dichotomy of direct and imitated speech, and indeed this brings us slightly closer to a dichotomy through which we can begin to examine Kate Grenville's deception. Traditionally, the terms used to enact this dichotomy are mimesis and diegesis, where 'mimesis is the mode of the drama and diegesis that of the dithyramb, or pure lyric expression' (p. 97). In broader narratological thinking, the term diegesis has evolved to constitute 'the (fictional) world in which the situations and events narrated occur' in addition to its original definition of 'telling, recounting...enacting' (Prince, 2003, p. 20). The logical question remains, however: who is doing this telling? To what extent can the reader imbue this 'teller' with a suitable degree of reliability?

A rather simplistic answer to these questions is that, of course, a narrator is present; according to Chatman, "the narrator comes into existence when the story is made to seem a demonstrable act of communication. If the audience feels that it is in some sense spoken *to* ... then the existence of a teller must be presumed". (2004, p. 98) This difference between narrator and teller is, of course, one of the central concepts in defining Curated Fiction; in *Last Orders* we presume that the individual characters are our tellers—until we consider we that someone (a fused entity representing, perhaps, Author/Narrator) has sequenced each of the accounts provided in a particular way, and further that the same entity has allowed Amy's truncated account towards the end of the novel to remain so; similar principles apply to *As I Lay Dying*. *Waterland* is an exception in that it makes use of a single teller, Tom Crick, but is narratively complicated by shifts in time and voice—a genuinely polyphonous work, in which the Author significantly maintains the illusion of absence and the Reader is able to sustain the impression that the events of that novel, including its many digressions, are occurring before their very eyes. It is clear, according to Chatman, that "the author must make special efforts to preserve [that] illusion" (2004, p. 98).

Which brings me back to *A Room Made of Leaves* and the consideration of Grenville's artful deception. This may seem a provocative term, but it's one that I believe is accurate with regard to my positioning of the novel as a non-example of Curated Fiction, and is to be found in the use of a contextual framing device. On some consideration, of course, all fiction is a form of deception of sorts—this is suggested by the very act of inviting readers to suspend their disbelief; the storyworld of a novel, no matter how grittily realistic it might seem or how accurate in its representation of real people living their lives in highly relatable circumstances, can only be illusory. This is perhaps especially so with historical fiction, where emotional depth or resonance is offered alongside whatever degree of historical veracity the novelist has been able to draw from research. (In other words, the historian will illustrate what happened, and perhaps why; the novelist will additionally explain how it felt to be there—an element of the historical narrative, you may recall, that is not generally available in historical sources or records.) Grenville's framing device begins with an 'Editor's Note' at the beginning of the novel that serves to make absolutely clear, firstly, that the contents of a box found in the roof are Elizabeth Macarthur's handwritten memoirs:

> The box—jammed with hard-to-read old papers, cross-written to save space—was somehow, unbelievably, mislaid until recently, when through a chain of events so unlikely as to seem invented it came into my hands. … In these private papers, written near the end of her life, she steps out from behind the bland documents that were her public face. They're a series of hot outpourings, pellets of memory lit by passionate feeling. With sometimes shocking frankness, they invite us to see right into her heart.
>
> (Grenville, 2020, p. 1)

There are some delicious touches of the gifted writer's art here: 'through a chain of events so unlikely as to seem invented' is perhaps the most mischievous claim, and indeed arrives more subtly than the novel's epigraph mentioned previously. However, the invitation 'to see right into her heart' succinctly captures Grenville's aesthetic project for this novel—to create a character in Elizabeth Macarthur that is fully on display for the reader, a frank and intimate portrait of someone who had previously remained largely invisible or at least little-known. Secondly, later in this 'Editor's Note', Grenville (who signs from this Note as 'Transcriber and Editor') tells us:

> I've done nothing more than transcribe the papers that were in the box. Of course I had to use my imagination where the faded old ink was impossible to read, and I spent considerable time arranging the fragments in what judged to be the best order, *but beyond that I've let Elizabeth Macarthur tell her own story.*
>
> (Grenville, 2020, p. 4; italics mine.)

With which, we embark on a vivid, beautifully written account of the life of this woman—her early years, her marriage to an impossible husband, a harrowing journey to New South Wales then still in its colonial infancy, her attempts to make life in this new colony on the other side of the world bearable for herself and those around her. And we might believe, furthermore and despite that stubborn epigraph, that this account is a transcribed primary source. All is revealed in the Author's Note at the end of the book:

> … there was no box of secrets found in the roof of Elizabeth Farm. I didn't transcribe and edit what you're just read. I wrote it. But this story follows the events and people who emerge from the letters, journals and official documents of the early years of the colony of New South Wales. The extracts from her letters that 'Elizabeth Macarthur' quotes are from the letters of the real Elizabeth Macarthur. I've taken some liberties in order to shape this work of fiction. The passage of time and the order of some events have become a little slithery in my hands… This book isn't history. At the same time, it's not pure invention.
>
> (Grenville, 2020, p. 319)

The old Australian expression 'having two bob each way' springs to mind with those last two sentences; Grenville is content to back both horses, history and fiction, in the race to neatly categorise *A Room Made of Leaves*. However, ostensibly, the novel defies simple classification; it blends both, although the extent to which they are mutually exclusive creates an argument beyond the aims and purpose of this book. In her emphatic denial of the novel as history, though, I detect a thumb of the nose at those historians who took her to task regarding *The Secret River* and one can't help wondering whether *A Room Made of Leaves* was intended to be Grenville's 'last word' on the matter.

Placing the history/fiction discussion to one side, we return to the framing device of this novel as a device which precludes the work from consideration as an example of Curated Fiction. It is a truism that magicians must never reveal their secrets, and effectively with the Author's Note cited above this is exactly what Grenville does. This is not to deny how artful and compelling the novel is—Grenville breathes energetic, exasperating, poetic life into her creation and proves once again why she is one of Australia's most celebrated novelists. However, in revealing herself as the Author at the end of the novel, she explicitly undoes the illusion she has created, revealing that—despite her exquisite characterisation of Macarthur—we were in Grenville's presence all along. Having initially established that the book is a work derived from a primary source, lovingly and diligently 'transcribed', Grenville sets up her storyworld on that understanding with the reader: that she is not making it up, that the words we read are Macarthur's. This is swiftly dismantled with the Author's Note and the reader is now faced with the deception that I mentioned earlier—that it mostly *wasn't* Macarthur's words they were reading at all. While there is some forereshadowing inherent in the epigraph, I can imagine that some readers, having been carried along on Macarthur's journey, would feel confronted if not slightly betrayed by Grenville's admission. Perhaps she is leaning into this revelation by Wayne Booth: "We must never forget that although the author can to some extent choose his disguises, he can never choose to disappear". (Booth, 1983, p. 20) Curated Fiction is premised on the notion that the illusion of such disappearance is very carefully crafted.

Conclusion

By stepping out of the shadows of her creation to reveal herself as the Author, Kate Grenville achieves two things—she complicates the interface between history and fiction (especially with regard to where a boundary between the two might exist), and she reinforces some core narratological theory—that all fiction has an Author. Someone has put words on the page. Very often, the joy of reading lies in being allowed to forget such a notion, to be swept along and immersed into the storyworld and the conflicts and passions of its various characters. Curated Fiction makes such immersion possible through various techniques; it displaces the Author and in doing so establishes a 'hermetically sealed' storyworld that exists without apparent evidence of invention. *A Room Made of Leaves* works sharply against these concepts by making the act of its invention absolutely and explicitly evident.

Note

1 Please note that I describe this as an attempted genocide, because the attempt failed; today's palawa communities in lutruwita/Tasmania are vibrant, politically active, and generous in their sharing of cultural knowledge. A treaty process is under way with the current state government.

Foxes

By *Cameron Hindrum*

The ceremony of innocence is drowned...

(WB Yeats, 'The Second Coming')

There is a great and mighty Owl in the corner of the room. At once I observe and ignore him creeping in behind the other boys, not avoiding his capturing gaze but trying not to notice it either. When I take time to observe, there is in fact a coterie of owls: dark creamed hair and darker eyes, brooding along the back wall of the room, in thin ties and loose cardigans, leaning loose against the wall and desperately trying to look as though they wanted to be anywhere else. I have forgotten the names of the others, such tiny men they were; one of them was Myers I think. None of them was worthy of the Owl.

The room is at the top of the stairs and it is small but I can see other doorways through the smoke, two of them, one door open and the other closed and the Owl stands next to the closed one, his arms across his chest and a girl leaning on him. She looks bored. The room is crowded with other people; it is dim and smoky and the air in the room cushions me somehow. I am already soft with drinking too much and I must steady myself with a hand on Derrek's shoulder as we enter. There is so much noise but it is quiet, people talking and laughing and somewhere I can hear a guitar, unassembled chords that sound like jazz and a couple of people tumbling drunkenly through vowels and consonants that I gather is supposed to constitute scat. Several people, perhaps half a dozen, are dancing and struggling, their elbows pinned into them so as not to stab anyone and how funny they look, danacing where there's no room to do it properly, confined to themselves but doing it anyway because they want to and I find myself thinking that I would not have the courage. I do not want to dance. I am inside the room now and the majestic creature watches watches watches me from the moment I enter and that is Him I say to myself, the beautiful poet. The lordly Owl, watching me and waiting for I don't know what. That is Ted Hughes. The room is warm but it is deep winter outside and I notice that I am shivering. In the presence of an Owl I suppose that that is what mice do. I will talk to him but I cannot possibly. I am drunk and I will sound like a fool.

What if I had not come to this place? I am, at times, the target of curiousity. People will watch me, fawning over the apparent intrigue of my Amherst accent. At times I cannot bear it.

Earlier: I was cold, staring through the pale smoke of the Yard, waiting for Hamish to return from the lavatory. They were expecting me to go and I concluded that I should not disappoint them. I held my breath against the smoke. Hamish was a very long time relieving himself. The Yard smelled of whiteness like the moon. Hamish emerged out of the smoke, finally, nervous and smiling. 'Heartbreak Hotel' plays somewhere, since my baby left me, how I loathed it. I loathed it but I would sleep with Elvis. I will finish my beer, Hamish said, and we'll go up and I think I remember smiling. We should go. The smoke was stinging my eyes. I was so tired of being the world's whore.

Would you like a drink, he said to me. A brandy please. He vanished again, into the smoke. The Yard was nearly empty, perhaps not surprising for a Sunday night, and if it were not for the party upstairs it would certainly have closed by now, I thought. I was bored. Hamish had agreed to meet Derrek. I loathed Derrek but we were waiting for him.

How I must stop using that word. It is not true and I must not be unkind, to Mother or Father or to every man I meet who cannot be Father. The world is not full of loathing. Why did you? With your one black shoe. I reminded myself that I should write to her tomorrow, or this week, as I'd had three letters from her now and I had not replied to them. I'm sure she does not wait by the letterbox for news from Me, but still. I must be a Good Girl. Mother saved me and I should be eternally grateful, a mushroom bursting forth from its softening soil, dumb and perfect.

'I don't know whether I will go,' I said to Hamish and he looked at me with those eyes. Perhaps I would sleep with him.

'Go?' He looked at me as if I'd said something impossible.

'To the party.'

'Sylvia, the committee is there. They will want to meet you.'

'Why?'

He looked down at his drink. I knew he was searching for a reason, having been pushed to find one. Men are so ridiculous some times. 'Because they like your accent.'

I looked at him. He was not smiling.

'My accent,' I said.

'Yes.'

'Don't be absurd.'

He winced. At the prospect that I might actually leave he looked utterly afraid and I could have done it then, walked out of the Yard and left him to offer some inept excuse or other for my absence, left him looking afraid because in the end perhaps that is all men are worth but I did not do it, leave him there like a child, stumbling over his thoughts.

I frighten myself at times with how mean I can be and it is fear that pulls me back from doing things. Perhaps it was fear, under the house in the dust and the dank shadows while they searched for me by the river and through the park and door to door. Perhaps fear kept me alive. I don't like to remember.

Derrek was late and so Hamish and I had to chat about God knows what, his fascination with Ezra Pound perhaps. Pound is far too clever for his own good, that's what I have said to Hamish many times, and every time I say it Hamish looks hurt, as though I have stabbed him. Hamish has a lovely boy's eyes. I do not entirely mean it not as a criticism—Pound was capable of innovation I suppose. But, villian that I am, how I enjoyed the withdrawal of his confidence at my words. The power I have over him. How I hate myself for enjoying it. I shall never find a husband or I shall find too many and neither of these positions is desirable. If only I could write children like a poem.

He returned from the bar with my brandy and I was already rather drunk so I made a rough estimate of the position of my mouth and it seemed that I was lucky. I was keeping an eye on the door for Derrek.

I would not sleep with Hamish.

The song changed. 'Smoke Gets in Your Eyes' and I tap my fingers in some sort of time against the blue pleat of my skirt. Hamish did not speak further and I hated him for being silent. Apparently I was not even worth small talk and we waited in the cloud of the music and the smoke while I watched the door on the other side of the Yard. Earlier, we had been at the Miller's Croft and I'd enjoyed three glasses of brandy there. I rather like brandy and will not at the moment drink anything else.

I shook my head and took another swill, to let him know that I would not make things awkward for him. I gave him a little smile. My world then was nothing but affectation. He finished the rest of his drink and looked at the large watch on his ridiculous wrist. It was a thin wrist, too thin, emerging from the sleeve of his pale cardigan. 'He's late,' Hamish said.

I don't say anything.

Derrek wrote sestinas and sometimes I think that if you are stupid enough to write sestinas you should be given a chance socially. We'd rejected two of them for the magazine but actually I didn't mind them, clumsiness of the form aside. He knew when to end a line. Derrek was taller than Hamish but still shorter than me and he has a moustache that I wished he would shave but he had refused up until then. It was eight thirty and I'd had too many brandies and Hamish put down his glass and glided his soft hands into his pockets. I said to myself: five minutes. If Derrek does not come in five minutes I will go back to my room to read Racine before I go to sleep and perhaps make a start on the paper I have to write before Wednesday, and I will not look back to see Hamish's wounded face as I leave.

I did not like to think that Racine would have been preferable company, but I thought it none the less. The brandies softened any urge I might have had to chide myself for my cruelty.

'Ted will be there,' Hamish said.

'Who?'

'Ted. You know, the poet I told you about.'

'Hughes?'

'Yes.'

Did he watch my eyes in that moment, standing near the bar of Falcon Yard? I don't know. Hamish could not possibly know how I had surged when reading his poems: earlier again, that day, Bertie was selling copies of the Review from a table in the courtyard near my room.

'St Botolph's Review,' I'd said to him, my hands in my pockets out of the winter. 'Is that a parish magazine of some sort?'

He laughed. 'Not at all love,' he said, in that charming English way that I sometimes found slightly cloying. 'It's poetry. Two shillings.'

I counted out some of the strange English money and flicked through the magazine there in the courtyard. I opened it at a poem called 'Fallgrief's Girl-Friends' and I shivered at the first several lines: not from the cold.

Not that she had no equal, not that she was
His before flesh was his or the world was;
Not that she had the especial excellence
To make her cat-indolence and shrew-mouth
Index to its humanity.

I said these words aloud to myself there in the bitter morning of the courtyard and I said them again aloud as I walked back to my room and by the time I closed my door against the world I had learned them. Hamish came by later, knocking slowly as he does, and I showed the magazine to him. Oh yes, he said, there's a party for that crowd tonight. You should come.

I should not have come.

And now we were back in the Yard, waiting for ridiculously tardy Derrek. Hamish was still issuing words at me.

'He wants to meet you,' Hamish said. He looked at his watch again. His hair was not perfect enough.

'Why?'

Hamish shrugged.

And finally there was Derrek, slovenly and late, scarfed against winter and reaching out to us, actually reaching, rather than saying he was sorry. Apparently he'd missed a bus and I wondered whether I should believe this when Hamish said that we should get a move on. How long the winter had been, how eternal and damned and I always reached the point where I did not think I would survive it. I do not like being cold and yet tonight I am not dressed appropriately, because I thought that we would be inside and that it wouldn't matter. I'd presumed there would be dancing.

But how the cold reaches in, how it always finds me, leaving out the biscuits and milk for them and sitting in the kitchen, staring at the cooker with the tick tick tick from the clock in the hall, and the damned cold and silence. I should not talk about time or how I do not trust it.

Derrek arrived a minute too early and I slightly hated him for it, but I should not be so harsh; at least I did not have to test my fear, yet again.

'I haven't finished my brandy,' I said to Hamish. He had already taken several steps away from me, taking Derrek by the elbow and perhaps telling him how exciting he considered the sestina to be as a form and then they both stopped and turned and looked at me while I took another sip.

'We're late,' Derrek said.

'I don't want to go.' I found myself saying it—I cannot explain why. What is there in a moment that we can describe as motivation? I have no reason. I think that reason has no place in the soul of someone who desperately wants to create, to be an artist. My thoughts are always so crowded.

Hamish opened his mouth and I watched him gawping at me like a dying fish. Sylvia, he said. Please. Derrek lit a cigarette and how I wanted one too although I had not smoked for some time and I did not care to start again. He looked at Hamish. 'Few minutes won't hurt,' he said.

I sipped my brandy and did not look at either of them.

On the whole, I enjoyed attending parties and Heaven knows there were enough of them at Cambridge in those days. Any excuse it seemed to behave badly and give everyone something to gossip about. But I had to be in the right mood to go to them and sometimes I could not have been further from it but still I was expected to dress up and chat happily as though I had been waiting all my life for the opportunity to do so. The other women are always looking at me. But it was cold and I had work to do, there was always work to do and what if I had not attended, what if there had been no magazine? It would be the first and the last. I hated the name of it, a pretentious Cambridge church name, named for the rectory where one of the owls was living. Always asking me, always on about Boston or New York, as if I had never lived anywhere else. I answer their questions and look at them and I ask myself is it you? Shall we go on a date and will we have babies and live somewhere warm and will you get diabetes and die? I do not ask these questions. Not of every man I am introduced to. Oh, I am so naughty and stupid.

What if I had gone home? To my room I mean, not home to Mother. My room is small and has a bed and I like it in the dark when it is small. In the dark when I am lying in bed I remember the walk I did not take, the note in which I lied to Mother. I crawled into the dust and shadows under the house and I waited for the darkness but it did not come and I drifted between pain and sleep for three days in the stink of myself and I called out to her, Mother where are you, and no answer. She was waiting for me to return from the walk with a smile on my face and some flowers in my hand that I stole from the yard by the Church, were they daffodils? They were yellow and in the shadow of my stink they looked sick in their yellowness. I had not taken a walk. I had taken too many but not enough pills and I did not die. A happy failure, found by Warren and taken to the hospital where I waited to get better while they electrocuted me and shocked happiness into me, thunderclaps of it, smiling voltage. You will get better, the thunder said.

Mother is still waiting for me to return.

If I do not go to the party, to celebrate this average collection of poems in the only journal they will publish, I will go home and I will not meet him. I will be good, getting a job and marrying Hamish or Derrek or someone else and having children. I will know what it is to be content. Is there not one such man who can spare breath for me, give me life? My children will grow up to be sensible and I will go for walks with them, leaving no notes behind. I wait for them to emerge from the smoke in Falcon Yard while the song changes again. 'Why Do Fools Fall in Love' and I nearly laugh with the silliness of it, the sweet boppy irony, the motherless stupidity.

Derrek gently grabs my elbow and says, this way Sylvia. It is my name, sounding like trees, and I go with him. I am about to cross the river and I do not know if I can swim but that is no reason not to try. On a stout branch on a large tree on the other side rests an Owl, imposing and majestic, with the deepest eyes. He writes the most exquisite poetry. Hamish is behind us and the three of us head up the stairs, apparitions of these faces in the crowd said the Fascist. I like Derrek's hand on my elbow but I should not like it and I know they all look at me like a whore. The stairs are narrow and there is Hamish treading lightly on the steps behind us as we go up, up, slouching towards Bethlehem, why I think of Yeats at a moment like this I do not know—my thoughts again, crowded and noiseless. I surge towards the party and there is a piano and dear Bert on his guitar, clumsy jazz chords with his sunglasses on, so bohemian even the smoke up here is bohemian, a different blue to the smoke downstairs. I should not have a cigarette. Groups of people are everywhere although there is not much room. They turn to us when we appear and raise their glasses and there is something like a cheer and there it is on the table, the tawdry little thing with its poems in it. Perhaps three of them are any good, other than Ted's. There is laughter and someone hands me another brandy and again I aim it towards my mouth. I spill some of it on the untidy collar of my blouse and Derrek turns towards me, pivots drunkenly and asks me whether I want to dance and I am drunk enough to say that I do.

I am turning in the room with Derrek and I am careful not to spill my drink as I dance and there is something like happiness in the room with me, next to me, outside of me. There are no thunderclaps and I am glad for the brandy and the silly guitar, dear Bert. How important we all wanted to be. Derrek does not watch me and instead he watches his feet and somehow he keeps in time with the rhythm, stepping backwards and forwards and kicking his feet out to the side and I am making no attempt to keep up with him. I stop dancing so that I can take a sip of my brandy and look around, lost in the cloud of chatter. I feel pretty but that is because I am drunk. Oh, that towering feeling, just to know somehow that you are near. People stop and stare and they do not bother me.

There is an Owl in the corner of the room, said the mouse, not hiding from the Owl's gaze. The mouse had been hunted, chased across the field, and all the while the Owl had kept its iron gaze on the tiny muscled body, running running running. Looking for somewhere to hide.

I turned away from Derrek and could see him again, taller than anyone else in the room, the only man who could be tall enough for me. He was not looking at me but I am sure he knew I was there and that now I was watching him. I was not dancing any more. Should I go to him? Should I be good? Should I drink? Should I wait? He was talking to other people and I could not see them. There were all of my breaths in my chest at once, pleading to get out and I know that my skin was flushed because how many brandys had I drunk now, I had lost count. You stupid stupid girl. And slowly like an Owl he turned his head, his magnificent large face in slow motion turning towards me and while I stood there he was looking at me and I wanted to eat him.

Did he say my name? Like a breath against my heart.

Take a sip and say something you stupid girl.

'*At dusk she scuttles down the gauntlet of lust,*' I said. '*Like a clockwork mouse.*' He tilted his head towards me. As he came closer there was something like a smile across that splendid Owl mouth—

'You like?' he said.

Oh god I had said as a silly little girl that I would never speak to you again but I am speaking to you now because here you are my divine Owl god right beside me as I drink and forget to dance with whatever his name is. You lift your glass while I lift mine. I never felt more like crying all night. I found my thrill. He was leaning into me, his face coming closer to mine, his lips and his breath on my cheek and he said something which I could not hear. I frowned at him and the words came against me, harsh in the small room.

'Vulpes Pallida,' he said.

I did not understand and I swallowed some more brandy. He leaned away from me, standing up again. Pale fox, he said. And then he was clapping his hands in time to the guitar, heaven only knows what Bert was playing but we were clapping to it and then stamping our feet and I felt as though the floor might give way. We would crash together into the ground floor of the Yard and people would be frightened and perhaps he would land on me, this vast feathered man, his talons reaching to tear me apart. The floor was moving with us. Clapping as happy as an idiot without the thunder, I was, full of the world of him and the brandy aglow in my stomach and then his hand was on me, on my hair and he had pulled away my beautiful red hair band that Mother had given me, my favourite and he held it while he clapped his hands and everyone was clapping. The hairband disappeared and I never wanted to see it again, my favourite colour from home across the water.

I would have preferred that winter could not end, I thought to myself, not dancing any more that night and the next day I would probably hate what I had done because I did not think he would want to see me again. There would have to be something else besides my loneliness.

We weren't dancing and I don't know what we were doing but then he grabbed me and pulled me to him and mashed his mouth onto mine and I could taste the beer on his tongue and the grain of his stubble and his arms were around me and we were for the very first time moving together and his mouth left me. He stepped away and I followed him into his shadow and I grabbed him this time and pushed myself into him and leaned my face up as if to kiss him this big man, the only one big enough for me, this mighty Owl: I brought my teeth to the skin of his cheek and I bit him. I felt the skin break as I pierced him and held him and there was his tender dark blood, the stuff of him, life force and his colossal rhythm, staining both of us. No longer a mouse, I drank of him, tasted of him. My mark on him now, the stink of teeth, fox-bitten. He no longer an Owl but my fox, sleek one, seed of my tenuous destiny.

There could be nothing now without him, and I had not wanted to come and I wished I had not come because I was scared of him and of myself with him. He gave me another drink and I swallowed it with him and we talked about his work and the silly little magazine and my poems, which he said he liked and everything was circling and going round, stars pulled into our gravity. The world dulled itself before us. I sat on his lap and swallowed my brandy and I could see my hairband on the floor, being trodden on and forgotten and when I turned back to him he was smiling at someone else. And where was the girl? The one leaning on him when I had entered the room, I could not see her and anyway she no longer mattered, not even worthy of prey. I would not leave him and I will not stay. More brandy.

As foxes we circled each other. Tempted into monogamy as foxes are. Recognising the sound of each other's voice.

6 Synthesis
An Analysis of 'Foxes'

Context: The Story

'Foxes' is the result of a mild obsession I have with the lives and especially the marriage of Sylvia Plath and Ted Hughes. I regard them both as major poets of the last hundred years and I am drawn to Sylvia Plath's work in particular as a synthesis of her enormous talent and her psychological profile—which is defined by the death of her German father Otto when she was eight, a suicide attempt in her early twenties and her descent into illness and mania across the last few months of her life, which culminated in her suicide in February 1963 at the age of only thirty. I am equally enthralled by the subsequent role that Ted Hughes played in managing her literary affairs; he arranged for the publication of *Ariel*, the collection of poems found completed on her desk at her death (although he removed some poems, added others and rearranged Plath's ordering); he destroyed her final journal and he would spend the rest of his life fending off accusations that his infidelity and desertion of her in mid-1962 may have exacerbated her mental health issues, providing yet another circumstance that could be factored into her suicide. In a letter to Plath's mother Aurelia written a month after her death[1], Hughes declared that he expected never to be forgiven—presumably for any role he was seen to have played in her decline and lonely death.

As with so many mid-20th century writers, we are blessed to have significant resources to hand in learning about Plath and Hughes—namely, their collections of letters, and in Plath's case her surviving journals as well. This is of course in addition to their work; Plath published one collection of poems, *Colossus*, during her lifetime, as well as a novel—*The Bell Jar*—which she published under the pseudonym Victoria Lucas (partly because she was concerned that her mother would recognise herself in Plath's less than flattering depiction of Esther's mother in the novel). Many of the poems in *Ariel* were written in the last 6–8 months of Plath's life—i.e., in the period after Hughes had left the marital home in Devon—and many of them are the poems for which Plath is now considered iconic—'Daddy', 'Ariel', 'The Moon and the Yew Tree', 'Lady Lazarus', and many others. Examining a writer through the prism of their work is one thing, of course—being able to glimpse a more authentic voice for that writer through their letters and journals is quite another. Reading Plath's journal entries relating to the period during which she met Hughes, including their first meeting, was revelatory—for their style and humour but also for the care Plath obviously takes in recording the experience as authentically and honestly as she can. (For this reason, we must frown at Hughes for his destruction of her final journal; ostensibly this was to protect their two children from the state of mind Plath endured during this period, although one has to assume that Plath was considerably less than complimentary about Hughes's character and behaviour during this period, making his decision in part an attempt to expunge his treatment of her from the record.) I read with delight the account of their very first meeting, which occurred a party at Cambridge to launch a poetry journal to which Ted had contributed, called *St Botolph's Review*. She records how joyfully inebriated she was, how keen she was to meet Ted, and famously how, having met him, she bit him on the cheek. He removed her hairband, which she never recovered.

All of these details provided the starting point for 'Foxes'. I admit to some audacity in choosing the write the story from Plath's perspective; in part I wanted to see whether this was even possible; I don't feel that I can make a definitive ruling on that matter although I am satisfied with the result. I will dissect some of the specifics of the perspective I created for Plath in the next chapter. The story's title comes from the obsession both poets had for animals; not long after meeting Hughes, Plath would record her initial impressions of him in a poem The Jaguar. Hughes's body of poetic work includes a veritable zoology—hawks, crows, fish, jaguars and, yes, foxes. There is an irony in the choosing of this title though; most species of fox have a reputation for monogamy and although this varies in some instances, some particular species (such as arctic foxes) are known to mate for life.

'Foxes' as an Example of Curated Fiction

Audacity aside, I will now examine the methodology of composing the narrative forces and influences that are at work in 'Foxes'. Traditionally, the reader may recognise that I have employed a 'first-person' narrator, that the events that occur in this story are related to the reader through an "I". This "I" is identifiable to the reader as the actual person known as Sylvia Plath; readers who are familiar with Plath's work or with some of the details of her biography will perhaps make some connection between that work and those details and the perspectives related to them by the "I" in 'Foxes'. However, this allows us to interrogate that "I" in a little more detail and ask some important questions: to what extent is 'Foxes' historically accurate? What has occurred in the space between my reading about the events of that night and the writing of the story—in other words, what imaginative forces has

Cameron Hindrum exercised in crafting the story? To what extent should the reader accept that the "I" in 'Foxes' is a reliable version of the Sylvia Plath who lived, breathed and wrote poetry? (In order to maintain clear focus on the analysis of creative writing as exemplified in the story, I will leave a discussion of its historical veracity to one side—suffice to say that the events as depicted are drawn from known auto/biographical sources, such as letters and journal entries.)

Firstly, let us explore the limitations of what is popularly known as 'first-person narration'. According to Wayne Booth, there is little to be gained from "a distinction that throws all fiction into two, or at most three, heaps" (Booth, 1983, p. 150). Booth argues that the classification of narration into first- or third-person, or degrees of omniscience, is necessarily limiting. Instead, he proposes the difference between a 'dramatised' and an 'undramatised' narrator (Booth, 1983). Broadly, an undramatised narrator may purely have the function of relating events of a story to the reader without necessarily being involved in those events—nonetheless, they have a role in mediating the story; in some cases, the undramatised narrator may be present in the story only as the implied author. A dramatised narrator is, as it were, inside the action; they are involved in what happens and may be developed in some detail as a character in those events (in addition to having the 'role' of narrator). On this basis, the "I" in 'Foxes' is dramatised as a narrator—directly involved in events, indeed to the extent that the version of Sylvia Plath who appears in the story is also its protagonist—the character who drives (or is otherwise responsible) the action of the story. (In this case, such action is construed as the meeting of Sylvia Plath and Ted Hughes; this is the climactic moment towards which the momentum of the story is shaped.) I must emphasise that indeed the 'Sylvia Plath' who appears in 'Foxes' is very much a version of this well-known person, invented for my creative purposes; we can return here to the notion of 'trust vs. truth' in Curated Fiction and the capacity of the reader to navigate between these two positions.

It is not necessary to read 'Foxes' with any existing knowledge of Sylvia Plath or Ted Hughes; enough is contained in the story to build up any required understandings of character and situation. The story does not aspire to be any sort of biographical account of either person. The challenge, perhaps, in focalising narrated events through a person with whom the reader might have some familiarity is to invite the reader (as happens in many works of fiction) to suspend disbelief—something which, in itself, is an act of trust. Put another way, the 'Sylvia Plath' who narrates the story may or may not accord with an individual reader's understanding of her, or knowledge about her. Broadly speaking, this can have one of two effects—either the reader will accord with the version of Sylvia they find in Foxes, or they might not. As the Author of the story, I am not responsible for either: I have crafted a character, who is also the narrator, for my specific purposes. It is not necessarily for me to decide whether the 'Sylvia Plath' in 'Foxes' is an accurate representation of the real person—I have made several decisions that might be considered creative liberties and these might not reflect how readers who are familiar with Plath perceive her. What *is* necessary for me to ask is this: is this character a credible narrator—is she reliable? Essentially, I have based my characterisation of her on three central premises, two of which (a and b) are factually accurate and the other (c) reasonable supposition: a) that she attended the party that night wanting to meet Ted Hughes; b) that she was drunk, and c) that she was working on a paper on Racine at the time and may have been torn between spending time on that to finish it, and attending the party.

Before unpacking some specific narrative methodology utilised in 'Foxes', it is worth returning to that oft-heralded advice in creative writing classrooms, mentioned in Chapter 1: *Show, don't tell*. This is a vastly oversimplified maxim that has some value perhaps in allowing writers to 'activate' their stories—by which I mean favouring action over narration. However, since we are dealing with the medium of print language when we consider the realm of creative writing (I will leave aside such formats as graphic novels, for the purpose of this discussion), we will eventually realise that 'showing' via this medium is not really possible; images and actions can only be conveyed by words, and are therefore to some extent mediated by a narrator—who, as I have established, may or may not be a participant in the events of the story and who may or may not represent a conceptual presence in that story known as the Author. In his seminal work *Narrative Discourse: An Essay in Method*, Gérard Genette concludes that:

> from our strictly analytic point of view it must be added…that the very idea of *showing*, like that of imitation or narrative representation (and even more so, because of its naively visual character), is completely illusory: in contrast to dramatic representation, no narrative can "show" or "imitate" the story it tells. All it can do is tell it in a manner which is detailed, precise, "alive", and in that way give more or less the *illusion of mimesis* [showing]—which is the only narrative mimesis, for this single and sufficient reason: narration, oral or written, is a fact of language, and language signifies without imitating.
>
> (Genette, 1980, pps. 163–4.)

The well-intentioned advice to 'show and not tell', then, is misleading; the concept of mimesis has its origins in Aristotle's use of the term to have a narrator present information *as* a character. In narrative storytelling, especially in print, there can be only telling—but of course we can disguise that telling very effectively and indeed one of the guiding tenets of Curated Fiction is that a writer has an array of tools, techniques and concepts at his disposal to do so.

There are two further reflctions on 'Foxes' that I will offer, which also connect the composition of this work to princples of Curated Fiction: interplay between fiction and truth, and the disnarrated.

Fiction and Truth

For this component of the discussion I return to earlier references to Umberto Eco's collection of essays *Six Walks in the Fictional Wooods* (1994). In the essay 'Possible Woods', he states that

> ...to read fiction means to play a game by which we give sense to the immensity of things that happened, are happening, or will happen in the actual world. By reading narrative, we escape the anxiety that attacks us when we try to say something true about the world. This is the consoling function of narrative ... And it has always been the paramount function of myth: to find a shape, a form, in the turmoil of human experience.
>
> (1994, p. 87)

I have contended consistently that Curated Fiction endeavours to blur the line between the broad domains of fiction and truth. It might be arguable that, indeed, fictional worlds must create their own frameworks of truth—this is required by a reader suspending disbelief. Where such notions become complicated is when a story presented to the reader as fiction is in fact based on events that actually occurred, as is the case with 'Foxes'. Anyone with access to Plath's Journals or Ted Hughes's letters will be able to verify that the events of this story occurred more or less as I have written; where I have overlaid these events with the techniques of fiction, the result becomes contested, leaving the reader to navigate or define the extent to which they are willing to accept the events of the story as accurately truthful.

Specifically, as I have stated, I have crafted a particular perspective, with its attendant nuances, from which the character Sylvia Plath is then able to narrate the events of the evening and, more importantly, her attitude towards them. However, with the aid of the most comprehensively written journal entries in the world, I cannot possibly know with any real accuracy what her actual state of mind was on that particular night; I know that she had a good time and I know from other contextual reading that she sometimes experienced reasonably significant mood swings and so I have merged these two broad understandings to create her presence in the specific world of that night, in that place. I have no doubt committed that ubiquitous writer's sin of 'taking some liberties' but I have done so in the interests of addressing Eco's 'paramount function of myth' cited above—to create shape and find form in what might otherwise be considered the turmoil of not knowing.

A somewhat symbiotic relationship emerges, then, in what we might recognise as the relationship between fiction and truth. One provides seeding for the other, to varying degrees; the (in)famous phrase 'Based on a True Story' at the beginning of films provides a rather umbilical connection between the two, of course; assumptions will flow from the words 'Based on'. To what extent is this basis in truth? More importantly, which elements of this story can I trust? As a subversion of the paradigm, the filmmaking brothers Joel and Ethan Coen used this phrase at the beginning of their critically popular film *Fargo* when in fact the events depicted in that film are almost entirely fictional. The navigation that a reader might undertake in determining truth within the context of a fictional storyworld is one of the essential and creative processes of the reading act—and in many cases, it is enacted by principles of Curated Fiction, of selective ambiguity and of crafting a narrative consciousness, which seek to delineate the parameters of that storyworld and the boundaries of its veracity.

The Disnarrated

Consistently throughout 'Foxes', Sylvia Plath makes reference to not attending the party that evening—what she might be doing instead, how her mood that night might have allowed her to remain at home working on a paper she had due, and so on. In addition, she makes extrachronological reference to events in a future that exists beyond the immediate temporal frame of the storyworld, namely her death. This alternative possibility—of what might have occurred but did not, or what will occur outside the boundary of a character's immediate knowing—draws on Gerald Prince's concept of the disnarrated, which he defines as "the elements in a narrative that explicitly consider and refer to what does *not* take place" (2003, p. 22, italics in the original). I visited this concept briefly with regard to *As I Lay Dying* in Chapter 4 but it is worth revisiting here in the different context of the storyworld of 'Foxes'. Let us be reminded firstly of the parameters of the disnarrated that Prince has articulated:

> I am thus referring to alethic expressions of impossibility or unrealized possibility, ... expressions of observed prohibition, epistemic expressions of ignorance, ... expressions of nonexistence, purely imagined worlds, desired worlds, or intended worlds, unfulfilled expectations, unwarranted beliefs, failed attempts, crushed hopes, suppositions and false calculations, errors and lies, and so forth.
> (Prince, cited in Dannenberg 2014, p. 306)

A concept such as this works with or sits alongside the manipulation of time that I have already discussed in this chapter. Ostensibly 'Foxes' is a story which occurs within no more than a couple of hours; of course it would have been entirely possible to contain the narrative events of the story within that frame. However, by considering what is disnarrated—what Sylva imagines, or would have preferred to have been doing instead, or what she remembers of her father (which itself is disnarrated since she has very limited actual recall of him)—I am able creatively to broaden and deepen the dimensions of her character and the significance that the events of this particular evening would have in her life. (To make further use of the phrase cited in Chapter 4, this also serves to "thicken and darken" the narrative texture of the story.) Furthermore, it allows for the completely imaginative possibility of an alternative life, one governed by choices that may or may not be made, as illustrated in this extract from 'Foxes':

> If I do not go to the party, to celebrate this average collection of poems in the only journal they will publish, I will go home and I will not meet him. I will be good, getting a job and marrying Hamish or Derrek or someone else and having children. I will know what it is to be content. Is there not one such man who can spare breath for me, give me life? My children will grow up to be sensible and I will go for walks with them, leaving no notes behind.

The narrative possibilities that emerge from a consideration of what *might* have happened but didn't contribute to an overall sense of narrative richness; they evoke, in part, the complicated nature of our own inner monologues whereby one lies awake at night reliving a conversation that was had earlier in the day and wishing one had said something else. I would contend that it is the presence of these possibilities in narrative that in fact *makes* narrative engaging and sustainable as a vehicle for the tellability of events as well as the recording of character. In part, the richness of this engagement in the specific case of 'Foxes' because it is widely known what *did* happen that night, that Plath and Hughes did meet and were later married, had two children and so on as explained at the beginning of this chapter. However, the craft of fiction allows us to go beyond what is known and what is remembered: it gives us the tools to explore potential alternative directions, or at least capture that integral sense of the human condition that often leads us to question ourselves and our choices. If (arguably) our lives are governed by an almost constant series of choices that we make, that take our days and weeks and years in specific directions as a consequence of those choices, it speaks to the richness and creativity of the craft of writing that we are able to explore what might have happened otherwise.

All of these factors fed into the creative process of writing 'Foxes', and in the next chapter I will further discuss and explore the practice of doing so.

Note

1 15 March 1963. In *Letters of Ted Hughes*, selected and edited by Christopher Reid. Faber & Faber, 2007. The letter continues: "if there is an eternity, I am damned in it."

7 Curated Fiction in Practice

Crafting the Narrative: The 'Triangle Principle'

This is my term for one of the simplest distillations of a narrative framework, consisting of three questions (adapted from the work of Mieke Bal):

- Who knows?
- Who sees?
- Who speaks?

With an omniscient narrator, the answer might be that 'the Narrator' (whether or not this entity is also the Author) serves all three functions; a homodiegetic narrator might serve one or two of them. Other choices will locate the narrative role of a story along the range between these two positions; a limited narrator might only have one function, whereas an unreliable narrator might have access to one and *give the impression of* being cognisant of the other two. Following on from this is the consideration of how the speaking element of this triangle will be enacted—homodiegetically from a subjective point of view, or with the inclusion of greater distance between events that are narrated, and the act of narration itself.

Consider the following sets of variations on these questions:

- Who knows, but does not (or perhaps cannot) speak?
- Who sees, but does not know?
- Who speaks, but did not see?

On their own, these variations can afford some very creative development of narrative situations and are worth considering or using as a storybuilding technique in their own right. Other permutations are also possible and can form the basis of experiment or play at the drafting stage of a creative work: Who knows, but did not see? Who sees, but does not (or will not) speak? Who tells, but does not know?

A second variation of this triangle principle is as follows:

- Who knows—and how?
- Who speaks—and why?
- Who sees—and when?

Exercise 1

Develop a simple story premise that involves a minimum of three characters: for example, Jack borrows Jim's car to take Jim's ex-girlfriend Angela on a date. Build some narrative complexity around this premise by adopting the triangle principle, which might unfold as something like this:

- Angela knows the car is mechanically unsound, but doesn't tell Jack.
- Jack and Jim have a conversation about Angela when Jack collects the car; Jack does not share this with Angela.
- Jack has lied to Angela about having a job.
- Angela has lied to Jack about her ongoing feelings for Jim.
- Jim follows Jack as he meets Angela and watches them.
- Jim does not know that Angela still has feelings for him.
- Jack suspects that Jim is up to something and does not trust him.

And so on. It is clear that a multitude of various narrative possibilities exist within this relatively simple scenario (and of course, involving other characters will only further this complexity). Further creative play is afforded by switching the role of homodiegetic narrator between the three characters; which of the three would provide the most interesting perspective on this narrative as it unfolds? (For the record, I'll go with Jim!) There is, therefore, ample scope using this technique to develop an apparently simple scenario into an engaging work of long-form fiction; you can imagine, also, that the 'web' of each individual character can expand to include family, ambition, history, secrets, betrayals, hopes and desires.

I will now briefly explicate two broad narrative concepts with a view to aligning them with the 'triangle principle'. The two central narratological concepts present in 'Foxes' are fixed internal focalisation, and free direct discourse.

Who Knows? Fixed Internal Focalisation

Fundamentally, this refers to the narrating character ('Sylvia Plath') being the mediating agent for the events of the story—that is, hers (and hers alone) is the perspective from which the events and situations of the story are presented to the reader. There are degrees of focalisation; by contrast, a non-focalised story (or one with 'zero focalisation') is one on which there is no mediating agent—the popular term for which is 'omniscient narration' such as we might find in the works of Jane Austen, Charles Dickens or Proust. Importantly, fixed internal focalisation creates some limitations—the reader can only be subject to the character's perspective, and things that occur external to that perspective cannot be mediated through the character's narration. In 'Foxes' I have manipulated this concept somewhat, because events that are external to the immediate storyworld are drawn into the narration; there is a flashback to Sylvia's earlier suicide attempt ("Perhaps it was fear, under the house in the dust and the dank shadows while they searched for me by the river...") and a 'flash-forward' to her eventual death, which occurs approximately seven years after the events depicted in the story: "But how the cold reaches in, how it always finds me, leaving out the biscuits and milk for them and sitting in the kitchen, staring at the cooker with the tick tick tick from the clock in the hall, and the damned cold and silence."

Fixed internal focalisation does not relate, then, to time—there are skips in time all the way though 'Foxes'. Rather, it implies that the narrating character is and can only be within the storyworld, and can only present narration that consists of events—and responses to them—that are directly perceived by that character. In part, this serves to displace the author; the narrating character is the teller of the story, and not (in this case) the author Cameron Hindrum.

The chief creative benefit from this approach is that language, perspective, attitude and to some extent style must all filtered through the agency of the narrating character; this may be a matter of asking, "What word would Sylvia have used to describe this situation/scene/other character?" This is an invitation to subjectivity; the reader of the story will, hopefully see the world through Sylvia's consciousness, or least the version of it that I have crafted. In turn, this reinforced the central 'character note' for my version of Sylvia: that she is walking into the event (meeting Ted Hughes) that will effectively shape the rest of her life, although she does not necessarily know it in the narrative present of the story. At times, she is reluctant, bored, acerbic, pleasant, convivial and detached—all of these qualities emanating from the representation of subjectivity that is shaped by adopting the character of Sylvia Plath as a fixed internal focaliser.

Free Direct Discourse

This term (and associated ones) relates to the representation of a character's thoughts; contemporary 'stream of consciousness' techniques are an example of this method although of course they are not its only possible manifestation. The term is broadly defined as "a type of discourse whereby a character's utterances or thoughts are (presumably) given as the character formulates them, without any narratorial mediation (tags, quotation marks, dashes etc.)" (Prince, 2003, p. 34). This method is most naturally adopted if the story is being narrated through an "I" or is internally focalised—it is important to remember, though, that a narrator can be an observer of events without necessarily commenting on them or providing subjective thoughts or opinions. (This would aesthetically present an entirely different range of stylistic options—more akin to journalism, perhaps, than the writing of fiction.) To illustrate how free direct discourse works in 'Foxes' and to make some comments on its use as a technique, I refer to this passage from the story:

> Would you like a drink, he said to me. A brandy please. He vanished again, into the smoke. The Yard was nearly empty, perhaps not surprising for a Sunday night, and if it were not for the party upstairs it would certainly have closed by now, I thought. I was bored. Hamish had agreed to meet Derrek. I loathed Derrek but we were waiting for him.
>
> How I must stop using that word. It is not true and I must not be unkind, to Mother or Father or to every man I meet who cannot be Father. The world is not full of loathing. Why did you? With your one black shoe. I reminded myself that I should write to her tomorrow, or this week, as I'd had three letters from her now and I had not replied to them. I'm sure she does not wait by the letterbox for news from Me, but still. I must be a Good Girl. Mother saved me and I should be eternally grateful, a mushroom bursting forth from its softening soil, dumb and perfect.

This passage allows me to differentiate between the presentation of judgment or opinion—as one might expect from a first-person narration—and the more genuine use of free direct discourse. 'I was bored', and 'I loathed Derrek...' are examples of the former, perhaps—these are attitudes or revelations shared with the reader and not necessarily known to the other characters. 'The world is not full of loathing' is also an opinion, although it is related in quite definitive terms as though Sylvia is reminding herself of an important fact. However, the two sentences 'Why did you? With your one black shoe', represent the use of free direct discourse. The short question and the reference to the black shoe are not connected, semantically or thematically, to any other utterances in this paragraph—they might strike the reader as a digression, anomalous to the otherwise steady and more or less consistent (perhaps even predictable) thoughts/reactions/attitudes that Sylvia is presenting in this moment.

However, readers familiar with Sylvia Plath's poetry might catch the reference to her poem 'Daddy' (which was not written until October 1962, well over six years after the events depicted in 'Foxes'). Central to Sylvia's psychological makeup was the death of her father when she was eight years old; Sylvia was considered too young to attend the funeral. Otto Plath had what may have been undiagnosed diabetes and had a leg amputated, hence the reference here and in the poem to 'one black shoe'. In the midst of her observations about the evening and the party and the noise and the company she is in, Sylvia's thoughts fleetingly return to her father—which is made possible to me as a writer through use of free direct discourse. In addition, the poem 'Daddy' conflates Sylvia's anger at losing her father so young with her anger at her desertion by Ted, who had by this time betrayed her with another woman and left their home in Devon to live in London. So the use of free direct discourse has two different effects—it allows me to capture a fuller sense of Sylvia Plath's psychological profile by referencing her father, as well as to allude to Sylvia's later poetic work and her use of it to address the complex and confronting emotional issues that had arisen for her.

Another example allows me to segue into the issue of time and tense as a marker for the shift between narrative discourses:

> ...but I had to be in the right mood to go to them and sometimes I could not have been further from it but still I was expected to dress up and chat happily as though I had been waiting for the opportunity to do so all my entire short life. The other women are always looking at me. But it was cold and I had work to do, there was always work to do and what if I had not attended, what if there had been no magazine?

Here, Sylvia reflects on her expected social duties and her attitude toward them; this is interrupted by a brief moment of free discourse—'The other women are always looking at me'—which is also marked by a temporary change to present tense. Again, this allows me to interleave an acknowledgement of Sylvia's psychological state (a mild paranoia in this case) through the narrative act, in a manner that I hope is relatively seamless—at least, seamless enough not to overtly disrupt the flow of the narration while still signalling some subtlety regarding the narrator's complex psychological profile. The change in tense also serves to delineate this sentence (a thought) from those surrounding it (memory).

Another of the creative benefits of such a technique is the flexibility it affords with respect to time. The specific events of 'Foxes' are fixed in time—the evening of February 25th, 1956—but thematic and metaphoric forces shift the plane of the story backwards and forwards, as previously mentioned. This might be described as Sylvia's narration being governed by forces of memory and foresight; although she is presenting to us the details of the event in which she is immediately and directly immersed, she makes clear and free associations with other elements of herself and her being in the world—from whence she has come, to which she might go. This allows an otherwise potentially linear narration—of events—to be 'opened up' and assume perhaps a more spherical (or at the very least, non-linear) dimension. Creatively this allows me to reference the known trajectory of Plath's life and to contain a sense of that trajectory—a span of over a decade drawn from within the events of one night—in only four thousand words or so.

However, the most significant feature of the characterisation of Plath is the extent to which she is able to narrate what she cannot possibly know.

Arguably this is the result of an authorial intervention on my part although I have deliberately not made it explicit—it is woven through the fabric of her narration in a manner that I hope is relatively seamless. The most significant moment in which this occurs has already been cited in Chapter Six, the brief sequence in which Plath foreshadows her own death by suicide nearly seven years after the events of the story occur.

Who Speaks?

As can be seen, then, developing a character-version of the poet Sylvia Plath who serves as the story's narrator allows for considerable richness with regard to narrative choices. Similarly, such richness is also possible in determining precisely how it is that Sylvia will communicate both as a character (ostensibly to other characters) and as a narrator. She is homodiegetic, in that she is fully involved in the storyworld from which she speaks; it is important that this does *not*, in and of itself, render her a 'first-person' narrator; it is entirely possible that Sylvia Plath could have narrated 'Foxes' homodiegetically as a third-person narrator. With reference to the aforementioned 'triangle' questions, however, she provides all three narrative functions, although as I will explain there are some variations that occur as the story progresses, especially with regard to the question, 'Who knows?' Because the narrative of 'Foxes' is subjective, the important second consideration is to capture the method of speaking—of tone, language use and style—in a manner that seems more or less natural or least in keeping with what is widely known about Sylvia herself or the events of the night depicted in the story.

On the one hand, crafting a character from a known person removes some of the creative work in terms of having to develop one's awareness of that character from the ground up, as it were; Sylvia Plath lived and was known and so her values, her attitudes, her points of view on many issues are also known and these have been adopted for the purposes of the story as they are reflected in her letters and journals. She does make comments somewhat critical of the sestina form in her journals, as she does in the story; brandy was her preferred drink on social occasions; she was intelligent and well-educated, from a comfortable middle-class background, and of course this will determine the specific language choices she makes.

In writing her as a character for Foxes and in crafting the regular interior monologues into which she lapses, I also drew on her poetry for inspiration and many of the descriptive flourishes she expresses ("I am already soft with drinking too much", for example; and "the majestic creature watches watches watches me from the moment I enter") might echo the lexical and linguistic constructions of her verse.

One of the fundamental considerations in crafting a character's voice in this way—or, indeed, using any influences or flourishes that are appropriate—is that it helps to create the impression that the reader is being spoken to—i.e., the character-speech takes on a quality of orality. We see this clearly in *Last Orders* and *As I Lay Dying*. Considered in this way, the narrative of 'Foxes' is essentially one side of a conversation. The intended effect of such a technique is engagement, that the reader will be drawn into the intimacy of the narrative situation. It further serves as a creative means to expose the emotional breadth of the character—frailties, doubts and fears as well as strengths and moment of victory. Irene Kacandes in her seminal book on this concept, *Talk Fiction*, makes effective use of the rhetorical concept of apostrophe to refer to a narrator 'turning away' from what is being witnessed to address someone who cannot or will not reply. I have adapted this concept in the crafting of 'Foxes' to allow Sylvia Plath to 'turn away' from the events of the evening in which she is participating, to address the reader—who, of course, cannot offer a reply as part of direct engagement in the storyworld.

Exercise 2

For the sake of convenience, let us continue to experiment with the Exercise scenario from above, the travails of Jim, Jack and Angela. Character and perspective (and to some extent, the seeds of action) will most be clearly (and efficiently) be established by how they speak, to whom, when and why.

  i Revisit 'Ray's Rules' in *Last Orders*, or Vardaman's one-sentence chapter in *As I Lay Dying* ('My mother is a fish.') Choose one of the three characters and write *their* one-sentence chapter, or their list of life rules. Distil the essence of their character into one utterance, or the list by which they choose to conduct themselves in the world.
  ii Considering the background, class, education and/or life experience of your chosen character, write a paragraph in their voice, conforming to appropriate grammatical constructions, vocabulary, diction and so on.
  iii Revise this paragraph to include some free direct discourse—remember that this may or may not match the choices of language construction you have made for the character. What are their hidden thoughts, memories, fears? To what extent does your character mythologise themselves? How can what be hidden be sustained or revealed (if/when it needs to be) by specific narrative/aesthetic choices?

As a result of this third task in particular, you should observe some complexity beginning to colour your understanding of this character. This complexity will open up multiple other narrative choices. How would they confront their fears? Why would they take significant risks to keep some things hidden? In what specific aspect of their life do they lack courage? Why? And so on.

Who Sees?

It is clear, of course, that Sylvia Plath is our 'tour guide' through and into the world presented in 'Foxes'—our fixed internal focaliser. She relates to us what she observes and the adoption of techniques such as free direct discourse allows me to share her thoughts, opinions, attitudes and observations with the reader as well. Leaving 'Foxes' to one side for a moment though, it is worth revisiting the other exemplar texts I have discussed and asking this question of those texts.

Waterland has a singular narrator, Tom Crick; we are ready to identify him as the one 'who sees' (and 'who tells' for that matter). The complexity of that novel's narrative design emanates not from a single narrative perspective but rather from the layers of time, history and myth with which Graham Swift constructs his storyworld. To coin a simple analogy, Tom Crick in that novel represents the pebble dropped into the still waters of a pond—ripples of narrative extend outwards from his telling, across time and (in the case of the chapters such as 'About the Eel') narrative language itself. As I note in Chapter 2, *Waterland* provides an excellent case study for considering how multiple narrative levels can emanate from a single source (the character of Tom Crick in this case) and the potential within this concept for ambiguity to become a central compulsive force in the crafting of Curated Fiction. In other words, Tom Crick 'sees' beyond the world immediately in front of him; the travails and vagaries of this world are related by him, through him, in multiple narrative ways.

Last Orders and *As I Lay Dying* share the technique that makes Curated Fiction explicit in terms of their narrative construction: multiple homodiegetic narrators. That is, there are multiple characters 'who see' in each novel and in each case those characters are inherently involved in and connected to their storyworld. In each case, this concept is pushed to the limits of narrative logic by the inclusion of a chapter that is narrated post-mortem—by Jack and Addie Bundren respectively. (This is a technique that partially inspired the capacity of Sylvia Plath in 'Foxes' to foreshadow her own future—something that, although she 'sees' it, she could not possibly know in the narrative present of the story.) As I have stated, the broad benefit of a narrative composed from multiple homodiegetic sources is in creating potentially contradictory accounts, contrasting perspectives, omissions or other forms of possible deception that enable the reader to determine who to trust or what to believe, thereby actively involving the reader in the unfolding of narrative events and their various possible implications.

An extension of this idea is contained in the question, in conjunction with 'Who sees?'—*what* do they see? To recall an earlier variation of this question, what is it that is seen but not told—and why?

There is a clear connection between consideration of this question and the importance of creating the illusion of mimesis—of 'showing, not telling'.

As I have discussed in Chapter 5 in strictly narrative terms there can only be telling, no matter how performative the writing may be or appear; however, the adoption of a homodiegetic narrator is perhaps the most effective way to generate an illusion that we are being shown what happened, rather than told. We are with Sylvia as she makes her way through Falcon Yard, being offered drinks, making small talk, chiding herself, wishing she had not come and so on; all of this unfolds before us as related by her; we can, hopefully, 'see' it happening alongside her. This construction allows for simultaneous exposition and illustration and as aforementioned it also affords the opportunity to create a rich character voice to enact the 'seeing', drawn in the case of 'Foxes' from multiple sources.

Exercise 3

Returning to our scenario involving Jim, Jack and Angela, imagine that Jack and Angela have discovered Jim observing them on their date, and confront him. Bear in mind, perhaps, some of the earlier observations you may have developed regarding the nature of the relationship between Jim and Angela.

i Write three brief accounts of this confrontation, one each from the perspective of the three characters.
ii Write a brief account of the same scene from the perspective of a witness who does not know any of the three characters. What observations would they make, and why?
iii Write an account of the confrontation from a completely objective, omniscient point of view, having access to characters' thoughts and reactions.

Which of these strikes you as the most engaging or interesting? What happens if you thread random sentences from each of the above accounts together? By all means, experiment with doing this if you wish. Remember that each subjective account may (or should) be defined by specific patterns of grammar, style and vocabulary—whether these belong an 'author-voice' or to an individual character. The result is most likely to be polyphonous, with some threads of orality, underscored by ambiguity—a generous measure of each of the vital ingredients in a dynamic work of Curated Fiction, fuelled by the life forces of creativity and voice.

Conclusion

I hope that what is presented in this book provides a helpful formulation for both the critical appraisal of works of fiction and for the development of creative work. I must reiterate that I have not attempted any kind of a universal approach to identifying or addressing the challenges that the creative writing process will summon: to do so is well beyond my expertise and would no doubt require a volume of significantly larger dimension than this one.

I will simply, in closing, reiterate some foundational principles: that Curated Fiction

  i enacts the illusion of authorial invisibility;
 ii enacts orality, the semblance of writing as speech, to establish character subjectivity;
iii invites ambiguity as a consequence of narrative complexity;
iv situates the reader–narrator–author relationship within an ethical context relating to trust and truth; and
 v enables a polyphonous approach to language and time.

As I hope I have made clear, there is no specific formula for the development of a work which utilises concepts of Curated Fiction; a single work (long or short) may feature some or all of the identified concepts, or it may feature only one. Regardless of its application, I hope that I have made a sound argument for the consideration of principles of Curated Fiction as tools for the enriching of both the creative writing process and the enjoyment of reading. The use of such tools opens up countless possibilities for experiment, play, revision and editing within the vital and dynamic process of creative writing.

In addition to the practical perspectives I have provided in the latter chapters of this book, I hope that ideas and inspiration will be drawn from my analysis of the four exemplar texts and the method and structure of their narrative composition; it is well worth asking, what lessons about the craft of writing does each of these novels provide?

In striving for innovative ways to tell stories and communicate character, however, Curated Fiction has one inherent and resilient possibility—to take readers, in Tennyson's phrase, "beyond the utmost bound of human thought".

DOI: 10.4324/9781032635477-9

Bibliography

Works Cited

ACHESON, J. 2005. Historia and guilt: Graham Swift's *Waterland*. Critique - Studies in Contemporary Fiction, 47, 90–100.

BABU, P. K. 2016. Words don't ever fit: Travails of articulation in William Faulkner's *Fiction*. Singularities, 3, 12–19.

BAKHTIN, M. M. 1981. The Dialogic Imagination: Four Essays, Austin, TX, USA, University of Texas Press.

BAKHTIN, M. M. 2013. Problems of Dostoevsky's poetics (Vol. 8). Minneapolis, MN, USA, University of Minnesota Press.

BEATTY, J. 2017. Narrative possibility and narrative explanation. Studies in History and Philosophy of Science Part A, 62, 31–41.

BLEIKASTEN, A. 1990. The Ink of Melancholy: Faulkner's Novels from the Sound and the Fury to Light in August. Bloomington, IN, USA, The Indiana University Press.

BOOTH, W. C. 1983. The Rhetoric of Fiction, Chicago, IL, USA, University of Chicago Press.

BOOTH, W. C. 2005. A Resurrection of the Implied Author: Why Bother? in PHELAN, J. & RABINOWITZ, P. (eds.) Companion to Narrative Theory, Hoboken, NJ, USA, Wiley. https://doi.org/10.1002/9780470996935.ch5

BROOKS, D. 2010. 'Ambiguity, the literary, and close reading. CLCWeb: Comparative Literature and Culture, 12, 2–10.

CHAMPION, M.G. 2003. Cracked voices: Identification and ideology in Graham Swift's *Waterland*. Critique - Studies in Contemporary Fiction, 45, 34–42.

CHATMAN, S. 1998. The Structure of Narrative Transmission. in RIVKIN, J & Ryan, M. (eds.) Literary Theory: An Anthology. Maiden, MA, USA, Blackwell Publishing.

CLENDINNEN, I. 2006. The History Question: Who Owns the Past? Melbourne. Black Inc. Books.

CRAPS, S. 2003. "All the same underneath"? Alterity and Ethics in Graham Swift's *Last Orders*. Critique - Studies in Contemporary Fiction, 44, 405–420.

DANNENBERG, H. P. 2014. Gerald prince and the fascination of what doesn't happen. Narrative, 22, 304–311.

DE GAY, J. 2013. 'What we're made of': Personhood in Graham Swift's *Last Orders*. Christianity and Literature, 62, 565–581.

ECO, U. 1994. Six Walks in the Fictional Woods, Cambridge, MA, USA, Harvard University Press.

Bibliography

EMERSON, C. 1997. The First Hundred Years of Mikhail Bakhtin, Princeton, NJ, USA, Princeton University Press.

FAULKNER, William. 1930. As I Lay Dying, London, Vintage.

FLUDERNIK, M. 1993. Second person fiction: Narrative you as addressee and/or protagonist. Arbeiten aus Anglistik und Amerikanistik, 18, 217–247.

GARVEY, N. 2022. Australian Journal of Biography and History, 6, 213–217. http://doi.org/10.22459/AJBH.06.2022

GENETTE, G. 1980. Narrative Discourse: An Essay in Method, Ithaca, NY, USA, Cornell University Press.

GRENVILLE, K. 2020. A Room Made of Leaves. Melbourne. Text Publishing.

GRENVILLE, K. 2006. Interview with Ramona Koval, ABC Radio National. https://www.abc.net.au/listen/radionational/archived/booksandwriting/kate-grenville/3629894#transcript

GUEST, C. 2020. Contemporary historical fiction and Kate Grenville's *A Room Made of Leaves*. Antipodes: A North American Journal of Australian Literature, 34, 200–216.

HANSEN, P. K. 2007. Reconsidering the unreliable narrator. Semiotica, 165, 227–246.

HINDRUM, Cameron. 2021. Foxes, short story manuscript.

KACANDES, Irene. 2001. Talk Fiction: Literature and the Talk Explosion, Lincoln, NE, USA, University of Nebraska Press.

KARTTUNEN, L. 2008. A sociostylistic perspective on negatives and the disnarrated: Lahiri, Roy, Rushdie. Partial Answers: Journal of Literature and the History of Ideas, 6, 419–441.

KAUFMANN, M. 1993. The textual coffin and the narrative corpse of *As I Lay Dying*. Arizona Quarterly: A Journal of American Literature, Culture, and Theory, 49, 99–116.

KONKOL, S. 2014. Traumatic and Narrative Time in Graham Swift's *Waterland*. "Hours Like Bright Sweets in a Jar": Time and Temporality in Literature and Culture, New Castle, UK, Cambridge Scholars Publishing, pp. 91–109.

LOCKYER, J. 1987. Language and the process of narration in Faulkner's *As I Lay Dying*. Arizona Quarterly: A Journal of American Literature, Culture, and Theory, 43, 165–177.

MENESES, J. 2017. Historical restoration, narrative agency, and silence in Graham Swift's *Waterland*. Journal of Modern Literature, 40, 135–152.

MERIWETHER, J. B. & MILLGATE, M. (eds.) 1980. Lion in the Garden: Interviews with William Faulkner, 1926–1962, Lincoln, NE, USA, University of Nebraska Press.

MULLAN, J. 2006. How novels work. Oxford, Oxford University Press.

OLSEN, K. 2010. Raveling out like a looping string: *As I Lay Dying and Regenerative Language*. Journal of Modern Literature, 33, 95–111.

PRINCE, G. 1988. The disnarrated. Style, 22, 1–8.

PRINCE, G. 2003. A Dictionary of Narratology, Lincoln, NE, USA, University of Nebraska Press.

RENFREW, A. 2015. Mikhail Bakhtin, New York, NY, USA, Routledge.

RUSSELL, R. R. 2009. Embodiments of history and delayed confessions: Graham Swift's *Waterland as Trauma Fiction*. Papers on Language and Literature, 45, 115–149.

SARTRE, J.-P. 2012. What is Literature?, London, UK, Routledge.

SWIFT, Graham. 1983. Waterland, London, Picador.

SWIFT, Graham. 1996. Last Orders, London, Picador.

TEBBETTS, T. L. 2010. Discourse and Identity in Faulkner's *As I Lay Dying and Swift's Last Orders*. Faulkner Journal, 25, 69–88.

TILLOTSON, K. 1980. The Tale and the Teller, Ann Arbor, MI, USA, University Microfilms.
TOLLANCE, P. 2008. Voices from nowhere: Orality and absence in Graham Swift's *Waterland and Last Orders*. English Text Construction, 1, 141–153.
WHITEHEAD, A. 2004. Trauma Fiction, Edinburgh, UK, Edinburgh University Press.

Works Consulted

BAL, M. & LEWIN, J. 1983. The narrating and the focalizing: A Theory of the agents in narrative. Style, 17 (2), 234–269.
BARTHES, R. 2000. A Roland Barthes Reader, London, Vintage, Random House.
BOLLINGER, L. 2015. 'Are Is Too Many for One Woman to Foal': Embodied Cognition in *As I Lay Dying*. Texas Studies in Literature and Language, 57, 433–463.
BRIEST, S. 2014. Morte Jack: The evocation of Malory's Arthur, Guenivere and Lancelot in Graham Swift's *Last Orders*. Connotations: A Journal for Critical Debate, 24, 271–289.
CRAYOLA, R. 2014. As I Lay Dying: A Reader's Guide to the William Faulkner Novel, Scotts Valley, CA, USA, Createspace Independent Publishing Platform.
DABASHI, P. 2019. "Too soon too soon too soon": Continuity, blame, and the limits of the present in *As I Lay Dying*. The Arizona Quarterly, 75, 107–130.
FITZSIMMONS, D. S. 2003. I See, He Says, Perhaps, on Time: Vision, Voice, Hypothetical Narration, and Temporality in William Faulkner's Fiction. Columbus, OH, USA, Ohio State University.
FLUDERNIK, M. 1992. Narrative schemata and temporal anchoring. Journal of Literary Semantics, 21, 118–153.
FROW, J. 2009. An ethics of imitation. Angelaki, 14, 77–86.
HATAVARA, M. & MILDORF, J. 2017. Hybrid fictionality and vicarious narrative experience. Narrative, 25, 65–82.
INGE, M. T. E. 1999. Conversations with William Faulkner, Jackson, MS, USA, University Press of Mississippi.
IRISH, R. K. 1998. "Let me tell you": About desire and narrativity in Graham Swift's *Waterland*. Modern Fiction Studies, 44, 917–934.
MILDORF, J. 2016. Reconsidering second-person narration and involvement. Language and Literature: International Journal of Stylistics, 25, 145–158.
MORSON, G.S. 2003. Narrativeness. New Literary History, 34, 59–73.
MURPHY, S. P. 1996. In the middle of nowhere: The interpellative force of experimental narrative structure in Graham Swift's *Waterland*. Studies in the Humanities, 23, 70–83.
PRINCE, G. 1990. On narrative studies and narrative genres. Poetics Today, 11, 271–282.
REITAN, R. 2011. Theorizing second-person narratives: A backwater project? in HANSEN, P. K., IVERSEN, S., NIELSEN, H.S. (eds.) Strange Voices in Narrative Fiction. Berlin, De Gruyter.
SMILEY, J. 2005. Thirteen Ways of Looking at the Novel, New York, NY, USA, Alfred A. Knopf.
VAN GORP, D. 2007. A Comparative Study of William Faulkner's *As I Lay Dying and Last Orders*. Dissertation, University of Ghent.

Index

Note: Page references with "n" refer to the end-notes.

Aboriginal people 63, 64
absence: active 40; evidence for 42; of inference 4; of language 48; as provocation 28–45; validation of 29; *see also* authorial absence
Acheson, J. 21–24
active absence 40
acts of curation 24, 49, 65
actual-author/curator-author 5, 7
advice: oft-heralded 82; well-intentioned 82
aesthetic distance 51
aesthetic-narrative choices 41
ageless spiritual ritual 39–40
ambiguity 8–9, 18, 22–27, 29, 35–36, 38
anti-narrative gesture 25
apostrophe 6, 92
Ariel (Plath) 79
Aristotle 65, 82
artistic licence 65
As I Lay Dying (Faulkner) 2, 5, 6, 8, 10, 22, 45, 66, 92, 93; anti-language of 46–60; context of 46–47; evolution of techniques 49–50; implied authorship 50–54; omniscience 57–59; physical gap 57; regret narratives 50–54; textures of voice 47–49; unreliable truth 54–57
Austen, Jane 88
Australian Constitution 62
authorial absence 1, 12, 19, 29; aforementioned illusion of 6–7; illusion of 4–5, 6–7, 27, 65–66; multiple narrative voices 46; orality and 12; sense of 12

authorial awareness 5
authorial consciousness 30, 39, 45
authorial intervention 5, 91

Babu, P.K. 56
Bakhtin, Mikhail 8, 19, 31, 47, 59
Bal, Mieke 3
Beatty, John 50–51
The Bell Jar (Plath) 79
Bleikasten, A. 56
Booth, Wayne 3–5, 51–52, 54, 57, 69, 81
Brooks, David 9
Bundren, Addie 59

Canterbury Cathedral 36–40
Carruth, Cathy 17
Champion, Margret Gunnarsdottir 13–14
Chatman, Seymour 65–66
Clendinnen, Inga 63
closed-loop aesthetic 30
Coen, Ethan 84
Coen, Joel 84
Colossus (Plath) 79
completeness 32
contradictory emotional states 26
Craps, Stef 33–34, 43
Curated Fiction 95; and ambiguity 8–9; case studies 34–44; defined 1–2; evident 23; and moral behaviour 32–34; narrative unreliability 3; and orality 6–8; and polyphony 8–9; in practice 86–94; and textures of voice 47–49; and tipping point 24–26; and unreliable truth 2–6, 54–57

Curator 3
Curatorial qualities 58

de Gay, Jane 32
dialogism 20, 24
Dickens, Charles 88
direct/imitated speech 66
discourses 8; double-voiced 14; free direct 88–91, 92–93; narrative 90
Dodds, Jack 29
Dostoevsky, Fyodor 8, 20, 31, 47–48
double-voiced discourse 14
dramatised narrator 81; *see also* narrator

Eco, Umberto 2–3, 64, 83
Emerson, Caryl 8, 47
emotional impediments 34
empathy 7, 10, 31, 44, 52
empirical symbol 27

Fallgrief's Girl-Friends (poem) 73
Fargo (film) 84
Faulkner, William 5, 6, 10, 22, 45, 46–60
Federation commences 62
first-person narrations 2, 4, 10, 12, 29, 37, 81, 89
fixed internal focalisation 87–88
flesh-and-blood person 3–4
Foxes (Hindrum) 70–78; analysis of 79–85; context of 79–80; disnarrated 84–85; as example of Curated Fiction 80–82; fiction and truth 83–84
free direct discourse 88–91, 92–93; *see also* discourses
French Revolution 22

Genette, Gérard 4, 82
gesture *see* anti-narrative gesture
Grenville, Kate 2, 10, 61–69
Guest, Charlotte 64

Hansen, P.K. 54
Hindrum, Cameron 4, 81, 88
The History Question: Who Owns the Past? (Clendinnen) 63
homodiegetic narration 8, 10n1, 46
homodiegetic narrator 86–87, 93–94
Howard, John 62–63
Hughes, Ted 79–81, 83, 85

implied author 5, 81
implied authorship 12, 50–54

Inglourious Basterds (film) 65
inner monologue 63, 85
intervention: authorial 5, 91

Kacandes, Irene 6, 17, 20, 21, 92
Kaufman, M. 57, 59
Kriakin, Yuri 47, 48

Last Orders (Swift) 2, 4–5, 6–8, 10, 28–45, 92, 93; analysis of 29–30; case studies 34–44; complexity of 32; context of 28–30; creating selves in 30–32; moral texture 32–34
Lockyer, Judith 49

Macarthur, Elizabeth 61, 64–65, 67
Meneses, Juan 24–25
Metcalf, Mary 26
Mildorf, J. 7
monologism 8
monologues 6, 30–31, 38, 85, 91
moral behaviour 32
Mullan, John 47

narrations: first-person 2, 4, 10, 12, 29, 37, 81, 89; homodiegetic 8, 10n1, 46; omniscient 88; second-person 7–8, 21, 49; simultaneous 53; third-person 10n1; unreliable 3, 5, 50, 54, 56
Narrative Discourse: An Essay in Method (Genette) 82
Narrative Possibility and Narrative Explanation (Beatty) 50
narratives: complexity 11, 20, 46, 48, 87; discourses 90; possibility 51; regret 50–54; unreliability 3
narrator: dramatised 81; homodiegetic 86–87, 93–94; omniscient 86; undramatised 81
Naval Memorial in Chatham 35
negative narrative space 25

objective author-self 4
oft-heralded advice 82
Olsen, Kathryn 54–55
omniscience 57–59
omniscient 'authorial' source 5
omniscient authorial voice 8
omniscient narration 88
omniscient narrator 86
orality 6–8, 24

Plath, Otto 79, 89
Plath, Sylvia 79–85, 88–93
polyphonous character-narration-language construct 48
polyphonous narrative structures 25
polyphony 8–9, 17, 19, 47–48
Prince, Gerald 53
protagonist 81
Proust, M. 88

Ranciere, Jacques 19–20
regret narratives 50–54; *see also* narratives
Renfrew, Alastair 20, 47
The Rhetoric of Fiction (Booth) 3
A Room Made of Leaves (Grenville) 2, 10, 61–69; context of 61–62; and historical truth 62–65
Rudd, Kevin 63
Russell, Richard Rankin 15, 17, 25

Sartre, Jean-Paul 4
second-person narration 7–8, 21, 49
The Secret River (Grenville) 62–65, 68
selves 56
semantic constructions 38
settlers 63
simultaneous narration 53
Six Walks in the Fictional Woods (Eco) 2, 64, 83
speech 6; direct/imitated 66
Stanner, W.H. 62
St Botolph's Review 80

stream-of-consciousness 49, 88
The Structure of Narrative Transmission (Chatman) 65
Swift, Graham 4–5, 7, 10, 11–13, 15–20, 22, 28–45, 93

Talk Fiction (Kacandes) 20, 92
"talk fiction" 6
Tarantino, Quentin 65
Tebbetts, Terrell 36
tellability 53, 85
text-reader interactions 6
third-person narration 10n1
Tillotson, Kathleen 5
tipping point 24–26
Tollance, Pascale 18, 30, 31, 42
trauma 15–18
truth 62

undramatised narrator 81
unreliable narration 3, 5, 50, 54, 56

Waterland (Swift) 2, 4, 10, 11–27, 30, 45, 49, 93; as anti-narrative 18–21; complexity of 21–24; context of 11–12; Curated Fiction in 15–18, 21; explication of trauma in 15–18; land/water duality of 24; as narrative 18–21; story as redemption in 12–15; tipping point 24–26
well-intentioned advice 82
whole-narrative concept 48

For Product Safety Concerns and Information please contact our EU representative GPSR@taylorandfrancis.com
Taylor & Francis Verlag GmbH, Kaufingerstraße 24, 80331 München, Germany

www.ingramcontent.com/pod-product-compliance
Lightning Source LLC
Chambersburg PA
CBHW051757230426
43670CB00012B/2330